To

_____

From

_____

Date

_____

10 WAYS TO DELIGHT
IN THE CLOSENESS OF GOD

always
near

ROBERT J. MORGAN

THOMAS NELSON
Since 1798

Published in Nashville, Tennessee, by Thomas Nelson. Thomas Nelson is a registered trademark of HarperCollins Christian Publishing, Inc.

Published in Association with Yates & Yates, www.yates2.com.

Thomas Nelson titles may be purchased in bulk for educational, business, fund-raising, or sales promotional use. For information, please e-mail SpecialMarkets@ThomasNelson.com.

Unless otherwise noted, Scripture quotations are taken from the Holy Bible, New International Version®, NIV®. Copyright © 1973, 1978, 1984, 2011 by Biblica, Inc.® Used by permission of Zondervan. All rights reserved worldwide. www.Zondervan.com. The "NIV" and "New International Version" are trademarks registered in the United States Patent and Trademark Office by Biblica, Inc.®

Scripture quotations marked AMPC are from the Amplified Bible, Classic Edition. Copyright © 1954, 1958, 1962, 1964, 1965, 1987 by The Lockman Foundation.

Scripture quotations marked CSB are from the Christian Standard Bible. Copyright © 2017 by Holman Bible Publishers. Used by permission. Christian Standard Bible®, and CSB® are federally registered trademarks of Holman Bible Publishers, all rights reserved.

Scripture quotations marked ESV are from the ESV® Bible (The Holy Bible, English Standard Version®). Copyright © 2001 by Crossway, a publishing ministry of Good News Publishers. Used by permission. All rights reserved.

Scripture quotations marked KJV are from the King James Version. Public domain.

Scripture quotations marked NKJV are from the New King James Version®. © 1982 by Thomas Nelson. Used by permission.

Scripture quotations marked TLB are from The Living Bible. Copyright © 1971. Used by permission of Tyndale House Publishers, Inc., Carol Stream, Illinois 60188. All rights reserved.

Scripture quotations marked THE VOICE are from The Voice™. © 2012 by Ecclesia Bible Society. Used by permission. All rights reserved. Note: Italics in quotations from The Voice are used to "indicate words not directly tied to the dynamic translation of the original language" but that "bring out the nuance of the original, assist in completing ideas, and . . . provide readers with information that would have been obvious to the original audience" (The Voice, preface).

ISBN 978-0-7180-8338-0

Printed in China

19 20 21 22 23 DSC 11 10 9 8 7 6 5 4 3 2

To Steve

Contents

Introduction

Imagine!

On a wet August night in 1964, my friends Sam and June Wilkinson waited to board a flight in São Paulo. They were traveling with three children, heading home for their first furlough after five years in South America. Four others waited for the same flight—four young men who were chatting with a group of women. Presently a limousine ferried the four fellows from the terminal to the plane. It returned for the Wilkinsons, and the airliner took off into the windswept Brazilian night, headed for its first stop, Lima, Peru.

Sam and June relaxed in their seats and helped the youngsters get comfortable. Looking up, they were surprised to see the four men coming down the aisle and gathering around them, wanting to meet their neighbors. Their easy smiles put the Wilkinsons at ease, especially when one of them pulled out a guitar. When they learned that Sam and June were missionaries, the fellows looked at one another and asked, "Now, what is that religious song we know?"

A vigorous version of "Swing Low, Sweet Chariot" ensued as the plane sped through the night. After the impromptu concert, the guys returned to their seats and everyone settled down for naps. Soon they arrived in Lima. The strangers disembarked for a connecting flight to California, and the Wilkinsons continued toward Savannah.

Only after their new friends left the plane did Sam and June, who had been rather isolated, learn the identity of the fellows with floppy hair and easy smiles. My friends had been traveling with John, Paul, George, and Ringo—the Beatles—who were headed to California for their second electrifying tour of the United States.

Imagine! Sharing a private, high-altitude concert with the Fab Four without realizing who they were! June told me she later wondered if she could have put her boys through college had she gotten pictures and autographs. Yet the memory is priceless, and June enjoys telling the story to this day.[1]

Talk about rare air. Sometimes we don't know with whom we're traveling. It's incredible to contemplate the possibility of being in the presence of glory and grandeur and greatness without realizing the significance of the moment.

As June told her story, I thought of another man who took a journey without realizing with whom he traveled. In Genesis 28, a man named Jacob was in trouble and running from home after cheating his father and brother. He reached a certain place in the desert and stopped for the night. Resting his head on a stone, Jacob had the most vivid dream of his life—a vision of a stairway from earth to heaven, with the angels of God ascending and descending on it. Above it stood God Almighty, who said, "I am the LORD, the God of your father Abraham and the God of Isaac. I will give you and your descendants the land on which you are lying" (Genesis 28:13).

> Sometimes we don't know with whom we're traveling.

The Lord reaffirmed the unbreakable promises previously given to Abraham, then God spoke personally to the young man: "I am with you and will watch over you wherever you go. . . . I will not leave you" (Genesis 28:15).

Jacob awoke and exclaimed, "Surely the LORD is in this place, and I was not aware of it. . . . How awesome is this place!" (vv. 16–17).

How awesome to discover the presence of God with us and

to say, "Surely the presence of the Lord is in this place, and I was not aware of it!" How wonderful to personally claim His words: "I am with you and will watch over you wherever you go. I will not leave you."

According to the Bible, God is nearer than we know. He is closer than we think. His eyes see us. His love encircles us. His presence comforts us as we lean into His nearness. Like Jacob, we often feel alone, outmatched by trouble, running from mistakes, overwhelmed. But we must remind ourselves that God is in the room. He is here, in this place.

You can relax in His presence and let debilitating stress drain from your nerves. You can cast your cares on Him who travels beside you. According to Psalm 16:11, there is joy in His presence. You can enjoy intimacy with God just when you need Him most.

Using a rich selection of scriptures, I want to show you how to experience the nearness of the God who made you, who loves you, and who wants you to encounter His closeness. The suggestions I'll share represent the habitual lifestyle of those walking with and enjoying the company of the God who said in Isaiah 41:10:

Do not fear, for I am with you;
do not be dismayed, for I am your God.

I will strengthen you and help you;
    I will uphold you with my righteous right hand.

Imagine! He wants to uphold you with His hand. He loves you, here, there, and everywhere. As you come together with Him right now by faith and see Him standing there near you, you can rest assured He's ready to give you all His love and grace. When you cast your burden on the Lord, He can work it out. He won't let you down, not on hard days or nights, not now, not ever. That's why our constant prayer should reflect the words of the old gospel song:

> *Just a closer walk with Thee;*
> *Grant it, Jesus, is my plea;*
> *Daily walking close to Thee,*
> *Let it be, dear Lord, let it be.*[2]

part one

delight

in Jesus

Just a Closer Walk

The town of Elizabethton occupies a lovely valley in the Appalachian Mountains of northeast Tennessee. It was a simple place in the 1950s, when I was growing up. My parents were schoolteachers, apple growers, and the kind of people who read their Bibles every day. I recall my mother singing hymns while doing housework. There was a chair factory downtown, and a loud whistle blew each night at ten o'clock to signal the shift change. The ten o'clock whistle also signaled my bedtime. My room was across the hall from my parents, and I often heard them praying before falling asleep.

We attended church each week, and I don't recall a time when I was not trusting Jesus Christ as my Lord and Savior. Some people can remember the exact date when they became Christians, but I cannot.

My elementary school was two blocks from home, and I was in the same class with the same children for six years. They were extended family. We opened each day with Bible reading and prayer.

I rode my bicycle to school and everywhere else. I was happiest when riding my bike up and down the hills in our neighborhood and all over town. My little dog, Tippy, rode in the basket with his nose to the wind, like a sea captain.

One week a preacher came to town, spoke of the death and resurrection of Jesus Christ, and urged the congregation to make sure we had truly received Christ as Savior. He invited us to come forward for prayer at the end of the service. I was too shy for that, but later that evening I locked myself in the bathroom and prayed something like this: "Dear God, I believe I am a Christian. But if not, I want to become one right now." I kept that experience to myself for years, but inwardly I felt a sense of assurance.

I kept a lot of things to myself. I didn't know the word *introvert*, but as I entered adolescence, I experienced introversion full force, especially in junior high, where, somehow, I never again saw my old friends. We were all dumped into the system. If the first decade of my life was idyllic, the second was lonely. I didn't

make many friends and, except for working in the library, disliked school.

My high school experience was better, because I went to a rural school where both my parents taught. They were popular with students, and that provided me some social leverage.

Upon graduation, I moved in with an aunt who lived near the college I wanted to attend, but she suffered dementia and no longer knew me. Because I lived off campus and was withdrawn, I didn't make a single friend during my freshman year. On one occasion I asked a girl for a date, which took all my courage. We went to see *Love Story*, the most depressing movie ever made. I asked her out again, but she said no. She was too depressed. As far as I remember, that was one of the very few dates I had before meeting and marrying my wife, Katrina.

I got a job at radio station WOPI in Bristol, where Tennessee Ernie Ford had gotten his start. I thought I'd like radio because I could talk to people without seeing them. But my career ended one day when everything went wrong in the studio. I was left alone without enough training. I missed commercials, messed up the ball game, played the wrong records, and butchered the word *appendectomy* while reading headlines from the teletype. The owner chewed me out, and I was so humiliated I simply never returned to work.

I felt significant loneliness that year, but looking back, I see it

was God's way of preparing me for a closer walk with Him. Once, for example, I happened to tune in to a broadcast and heard a preacher say God wanted to use us as Jesus had used the donkey on Palm Sunday. On another broadcast, I heard about the presence of the Holy Spirit within us. I can still quote parts of those sermons. I longed for more than I had.

One evening, while propped up in bed and reading, I had a distinct impression that I should enroll at Columbia International University in South Carolina. On September 2, 1971, I walked into my dormitory room.

Presently, two roommates showed up, Don Morgan and Bill McCoy. We had been placed in our rooms alphabetically. Bill, full of zeal, wasted no time in challenging me to offer God every part of my life as best I could. He told me God had a plan for me and wanted me to delight in His nearness every day. The Holy Spirit, Bill said, longed to flow through me. Bill picked up his guitar and starting singing. There were no air conditioners in the dorms back then, and it was a sweltering night. Bill sat shirtless on his bunk, legs crossed, strumming his guitar, and singing, "Just a closer walk with Thee, grant it, Jesus, is my plea."

Something clicked that night, and I knew that was what I wanted—a closer walk with God. The next evening I knelt by an old sofa and asked the Lord to take control of my life. Whatever He

wanted. Wherever He sent me. That night God flipped a switch of adrenaline inside me that has never shut off. I began learning how to live in God's presence, to enjoy His company, and with His help, to walk with Him.

In the half century since, I've had ups and downs. Life has been harder and heavier than I expected, and I've had ongoing battles with anxiety. I'm appalled at mistakes I've made along the way. But that "closer walk with Thee" is my lifeline.

I knew that was what I wanted—a closer walk with God.

As in a friendship or a marriage, we're either drawing nearer to God or drifting from Him all the time. Relationships aren't static. They grow richer or leaner with the passing years. It helps to remember how God longs to be near us, to walk with us, and to enjoy our company. In the Bible, He was always coming down from heaven to be with His people—with Adam and Eve in the Garden; with the children of Israel in a column of cloud and fire; with the nation of Israel in the temple; with the disciples along the lonely trails of Galilee; in the fiery descent of the Holy Spirit on the day of Pentecost; and with the apostle John on the island of Patmos.

I was nineteen when I knelt by the sofa in the dormitory

stairwell and yielded my life to Christ. Shortly afterward I found two Bible verses that became foundational to my relationship with God. The first was Psalm 139:16 in *The Living Bible:* "You saw me before I was born and scheduled each day of my life before I began to breathe. Every day was recorded in your book!" The Lord had planned every detail of my life, I realized, down to each day's schedule. My part was to say each morning, "Lord, what do You want me to do today?"

The second foundational Bible verse was Philippians 3:10: "[For my determined purpose is] that I may know Him [that I may progressively become more deeply and intimately acquainted with Him, perceiving and recognizing and understanding the wonders of His Person more strongly and more clearly]" (AMPC). The greatest purpose in life, I learned, is getting to know the Lord more deeply and intimately. I didn't have to be perfect, I realized, just growing in a daily walk with Him, even when it feels I'm taking two steps forward and one step backward.

While my story is unique to me, its general outline is familiar to everyone who longs to delight in God's closeness. At some point: (1) We establish a relationship with God through Jesus Christ, as I did, thankfully, in childhood. It's never too late to turn from our failures and receive God's grace. (2) We develop the inner assurance that we are children of God, and the Bible promises such security.

Perhaps you need to pray, "Lord, I think I am a Christian, but if not, I want to become one now." (3) We understand that requires a total-life commitment to Him: "Lord, whatever You want of me, I'm Yours. Fulfill Your plan for me." (4) We then embark on a lifelong experience of "just a closer walk" with Him, progressively coming to know Him more deeply and intimately.

Where are you in this process? Maybe your life is idyllic. Maybe you're lonely. Perhaps God is moving you toward a richer spiritual experience. Wherever you are, remember: every step begins with Jesus, whose name is Immanuel—God with us.

> *Just when I need Him, Jesus is near,*
> *Just when I falter, just when I fear;*
> *Ready to help me, ready to cheer,*
> *Just when I need Him most.*
> WILLIAM C. POOLE, "JUST WHEN I NEED HIM"

The Rabid Dog

Just when you need Him, Jesus is near. According to E. Stanley Jones, that's why we can relax in His presence. "His power cannot get across to you unless you learn to relax," Jones wrote. "Fear and worry tighten you up. Faith relaxes you. Often fear and worry keep the motor running even after you are parked. You are worn out even when sitting still. . . . You cannot repeat to yourself too frequently the oft-repeated, and yet always healing, statement: 'Let go; let God.'"[1]

Sometimes I'm as tense as a box of coils about to burst, but two Bible passages have shown me what to do on every occasion. The first is Hebrews 10:22: "Draw near to God with a sincere heart and with the full assurance that faith brings."

The original recipients of the book of Hebrews were veteran

Christ-followers who, earlier in their experience, had been zealous. Over time they had grown settled and complacent. A new wave of persecution seemed headed their way, and some were thinking of abandoning their faith and reverting to their original Jewish religion. The writer—we don't know his name—told them to draw near to God (10:22), for Christ, he said, is superior to everything in the Old Testament. Jesus is superior to the angels (1:4). He is superior to Moses and the law (3:3–6), to the sacrifices and priests (10:1–14). The writer went on to say:

> Remember those earlier days after you had received the light, when you endured in a great conflict of suffering. Sometimes you were publicly exposed to insult and persecution; at other times you stood side by side with those who were so treated. You suffered along with those in prison and joyfully accepted the confiscation of your property because you knew that you yourselves had better and lasting possessions. So do not throw away your confidence. . . . You need to persevere so that when you have done the will of God, you will receive what he has promised. (Hebrews 10:32–36)

Don't throw away your confidence. You need to persevere by leaning into God's presence. "Let us draw near to God with a sincere heart and with the full assurance that faith brings. . . . Because God has said, 'Never will I leave you; never will I forsake you.' So we say with confidence, 'The Lord is my helper; I will not be afraid'" (Hebrews 10:22; 13:5–6).

Life, even when it's wonderful, is challenging; every day has its own burdens. But whatever happens, draw near to God with sincere faith, for He has promised to never leave you. He is your helper, "an ever-present help in trouble" (Psalm 46:1).

The second passage is similar: "Submit yourselves, then, to God. Resist the devil, and he will flee from you. Come near to God and he will come near to you" (James 4:7–8). Here we find an additional fact. Drawing near to God requires resisting the devil. According to the Bible, Satan is a genuine personality of evil seeking to discourage us (Ephesians 6:11–12). But God will never forsake His children, so we must constantly flee our enemy and run to our Lord.

Drawing near to God requires resisting the devil.

This passage reminds me of my friend Harold Adolph, who grew up in China just before World War II. His father was a physician, and their city was under Japanese occupation.

"One morning when I was about seven years old and heading

out the door to school," Harold told me, "I heard my father mention the city was out of rabies vaccine and whoever was bitten by a
rabid dog would die." He continued:

> That afternoon I was walking home after school with my books.
> I had gone a block when I heard a fellow, very tall, coming behind
> me, running like the devil. When I turned to look, he said, "Run
> for your life. There's a dog coming." I thought he might have put
> me in a tree or on a wall, but, no, he just ran past, and now the
> rabid dog wasn't chasing him. It was chasing me. I threw down
> my books and ran as fast as my legs could move.
>
> I got to the corner and had to go up a steep incline for a
> block, and then another block to the house. The dog was getting
> closer, snarling and foaming. I was nearing the point of collapse
> when I finally made it to our house. I literally flew over the gate
> and fell in a heap on the other side. Gasping, I lifted my head and
> looked back. The dog was lying a few feet away, his front paws on
> the ground as if praying and his head resting on them. I thought
> he was getting ready to pounce. But he was dead. God made sure
> he died before he got me.[2]

What a picture! The devil is a rabid dog, pursuing us, wanting
to harm us. But Jesus said, "I am the gate; whoever enters through

me will be saved" (John 10:9). Furthermore, Satan is defeated, conquered by Christ through the cross and the tomb. How urgently we must flee the devil and draw near to God!

If worries dominate your thoughts, you'll be troubled. If Christ gets your attention, He will prevail over your mood and morale. Whatever you're facing, let go and let God. Learn to relax in His presence. Don't remain discouraged, but as Hebrews 10:22 says, "Draw near to God with a sincere heart." And as James puts it, "Resist the devil, and he will flee from you. Come near to God and he will come near to you" (4:7–8).

That's the doggone best advice you'll ever find on this subject.

God's Two Addresses

Years ago, Sophie Lichtenfels, a German-born maid in New York City, heard a sermon by Dr. A. B. Simpson and decided to follow Christ. Sophie lived in a tenement house on West Forty-Fourth Street, and much of her time was spent on hands and knees with a washtub and a scrub brush. She spoke with a heavy accent and wore a large bonnet with flowers. Her enthusiasm was contagious.

"God called me to scrub and preach," she said. "I was born a preacher, but since I was poor, I had to work. My work is good, and I can be trusted, so they want me. But if they have me, they must hear me preach. . . . I scrub as unto the Lord and I preach to all in the house."

Sophie had gone through a bad marriage with a man who had robbed her and vanished. But when asked about loneliness, she said, "How many in my family? Four—Father, Son, Holy Ghost, and me."

She continued:

> "I scrub as unto the Lord and I preach to all in the house."

For twelve years, I prayed the Lord to make me a foreign missionary. One day my Father said, "Sophie. Where were you born?" "In Germany," I replied. "And where you are now?" "In America." Then He said to me, "Who lives on the floor above you?" "A family of Swedes." "And above them?" "Some Swiss." "Yes, and in back are Italians, and a block away Chinese. You have never spoken to them about My Son. Do you think I'll send you a thousand miles away when you've got foreigners, even heathen, all around you?"[1]

Sophie had God's presence around her and His purpose within her. Her exuberant story showed up in newspapers, and she became something of a celebrity, always giving the glory to

God. Her cure for loneliness was her three roommates—Father, Son, and Holy Spirit—and doing the bidding of God.

Sophie must have known Isaiah 57:15, which reveals God's two addresses:

> This is what the high and exalted One says—
>> he who lives forever, whose name is holy:
> "I live in a high and holy place,
>> but also with the one who is contrite and lowly in spirit,
> to revive the spirit of the lowly
>> and to revive the heart of the contrite."

This verse reveals two beautiful things about God's presence. *God's presence is pervasive*; that is, He is everywhere. He dwells in a high and holy place, and His Being permeates the universe.

- "'Do not I fill heaven and earth?' declares the LORD." (Jeremiah 23:24)
- "The heavens, even the highest heaven, cannot contain you." (1 Kings 8:27)
- "Where can I go from your Spirit? Where can I flee from your presence? If I go up to the heavens, you are there; if I make my bed in the depths, you are there. If I rise on

the wings of the dawn, if I settle on the far side of the sea, even there your hand will guide me." (Psalm 139:7–10)

Fourteenth-century scholar Meister Eckhart said, "God is an infinite circle whose center is everywhere and whose circumference is nowhere."[2] Hildebert of Lavardin wrote, "God is over all things, under all things; outside all; within but not enclosed; without but not excluded . . . wholly above, presiding; wholly beneath, sustaining; wholly within, filling."[3]

This is mind-boggling, but isn't that what we would expect from an infinite God? His greatness is unfathomable (Psalm 145:3). Some people don't believe in God because they can't understand Him, but my faith is strengthened by having a God who transcends comprehension. The nature of the definition of *God* implies boundless, bottomless infinity. We might as well try to catch a hurricane in a hat as try to grasp the immensity of God with our finite minds.

God's presence is also personal. He isn't simply a force infusing the universe. He is a Person to know, a Friend to enjoy, a Lord to worship, and a Father who cares.

- "The Lord is near. Do not be anxious about anything." (Philippians 4:5–6)

- "Though I walk through the darkest valley, I will fear no evil, for you are with me." (Psalm 23:4)
- "My Presence will go with you, and I will give you rest." (Exodus 33:14)
- "As I was with Moses, so I will be with you; I will never leave you nor forsake you." (Joshua 1:5)
- "Surely I am with you always, to the very end of the age." (Matthew 28:20)
- "God is our refuge and strength, an ever-present help in trouble." (Psalm 46:1)

This was the message of Nicholas Herman, or Brother Lawrence, who was born in France in 1605. He worked in government until retiring to a monastery, where he was assigned kitchen duty. He hated the task until he realized God was as close in the kitchen as in the chapel. He developed what he called "that *habitual sense of* GOD's *Presence*."[4] As his attitude changed, so did his demeanor. Others began asking the reason for his radiance, and notes from his letters and conversations were cobbled into a book known as *The Practice of the Presence of God.*

According to Brother Lawrence,

When we are faithful to keep ourselves in His holy Presence, and set Him always before us, this not only hinders our offending Him and doing anything that may displease Him, at least willfully [sic], but it also begets in us a holy freedom, and, if I may so speak, a familiarity with GOD, wherewith we ask, and that successfully, the graces we stand in need of. . . . By often repeating these acts, they become *habitual*, and the presence of GOD rendered as it were *natural* to us.[5]

God's presence is pervasive, so God is infinite. His presence is personal, so He is intimate. How often, when lonely or stressed, I have drawn near to God, in Christ, through a verse of Scripture, a page in my journal, a few minutes of prayer, a stanza from a hymn, a passage from a devotional book, an encouragement from a friend, or some moments of biblical meditation.

We can learn something from a New York scrubwoman and from a monastery cook. We can learn to live with Father, Son, and Holy Ghost. We can delight in practicing the presence of the God whose business card lists two addresses—He both fills the highest heavens and dwells among His people.

part two

delight

in Listening
to God

Don't Be Afraid; I Am with You

As Jim Harvey traveled to Sacramento, his plane made a stop in Dallas. Before new passengers boarded, the flight attendant announced that a group of Russian immigrants was coming aboard and that, since they didn't speak English, they might need help and patience. Jim's grandparents had immigrated from Russia, so he watched carefully as a family came down the aisle. The man carried a child and led another. His wife accompanied two more youngsters. Jim felt compassion toward them and longed to be of service. The father stuffed his bags in the overhead compartment and took a seat across the aisle.

When the plane took off, the Russian looked at his watch, and

Jim noticed it was set to the wrong time zone. Reaching over, Jim showed him the correct time, and the man smiled and nodded. When the man took out the in-flight magazine and started looking at maps, Jim pointed to Sacramento and showed him where he was going.

A bit later, Jim stood in the aisle and extracted his brown leather Bible from the overhead bin. The Russian did the same, pulling out his own brown leather-covered book. Both men lowered their tray tables and began reading. "I could tell by the way the pages were laid out it was a Bible," Jim recalled. "I motioned for him to hand it to me, which he did. Although I could not read Russian, I was able to find Isaiah 41:10 by following the order of the Bible books and reading the numbers, which were the same as English. I handed the Bible back to him with my finger on these words: 'Do not fear, for I am with you; do not be afraid, for I am your God. I will strengthen; I will help you; I will hold on to you with my righteous right hand' [CSB].

"I watched as my new friend read these comforting words. He looked up with a countenance of peace and of gratitude."

Once in Sacramento, the new immigrants were met by a group of Russian Christians who lived in the area, and Jim rejoiced at the thought of God's constantly abiding presence with His people.[1]

Many years ago, my father gave me a leather Bible. It was a King James Version with tabs to help me find the various sections. In this way I learned my way around Scripture.

One night I found Isaiah 41:10 and learned it by heart almost instantly. I've quoted it thousands of times since, usually to myself.

> Fear thou not; for I am with thee: be not dismayed; for I am thy God: I will strengthen thee; yea, I will help thee; yea, I will uphold thee with the right hand of my righteousness. (KJV)

The background of the verse enhances its meaning. Isaiah contains sixty-six chapters. The first thirty-five are warnings to the people of Judah facing the Assyrian Empire in the east. Chapters 36 through 39 are historical, telling what happened during the Assyrian invasion and about the growing influence of the Babylonian Empire. Chapters 40 through 66 are addressed to the refugees of the Babylonian invasion of 587 BC.

The words of Isaiah 40–66, then, were written to immigrants and refugees, to those forced from home and driven to strange lands. These people, like so many today, needed comfort and hope, and these twenty-seven chapters contain some of the most encouraging verses in the Old Testament, including this great reassurance:

Have you not heard?
The LORD is the everlasting God,
    the Creator of the ends of the earth. . . .
Those who hope in the LORD
    will renew their strength.
They will soar on wings like eagles;
    they will run and not grow weary,
    they will walk and not be faint. (Isaiah 40:28, 31)

Isaiah continued in chapter 41 to explain that God had allowed certain things to happen to these survivors, which, in His providence, would work for their good. He told them, "I have chosen you and have not rejected you. So do not fear, for I am with you; do not be dismayed, for I am your God. I will strengthen you and help you; I will uphold you with my righteous right hand" (vv. 9–10).

When you learn Isaiah 41:10 by heart, it never leaves you. There are:

Two "Do Nots"
Do not fear.
Do not be dismayed.

Two "I Ams"
I am with you.
I am your God.

Three "I Wills"
I will strengthen you.
I will help you.
I will uphold you with My righteous right hand.

It's even better when you personalize it. I read of a Norwegian woman, Marie Monsen, who was on a ship seized by pirates in the Yellow Sea. "Just before daylight," she wrote, "I heard pistol shots, and I knew what we were in for. I was immediately reminded of the word I had been using much in years gone by, Isaiah 41:10, and I will read it to you as I had been reading it down on the Honan plains, 'Fear not, Marie, for I am with thee; be not dismayed, Marie, for I am thy God; I will strengthen thee, Marie, yea, I will uphold thee, Marie, with the right hand of my righteousness.'"

For twenty-three days, Marie stood on that promise and took every opportunity of sharing Christ with the pirates. She was finally released unharmed. Her captors didn't know what to do with a woman like her.[2]

I want to encourage you to adopt Isaiah 41:10 as your own personal scripture. Put your name in it, and take the Lord at His Word. Do not be afraid today. Do not be dismayed. The Lord is with you; He will strengthen, help, and uphold you with His righteous right hand.

Fear not, I am with thee, oh, be not dismayed,
For I am thy God, and will still give thee aid;
I'll strengthen thee, help thee, and cause thee to stand,
Upheld by My gracious, omnipotent hand.

ANONYMOUS, "HOW FIRM A FOUNDATION"

Finding Your Own Personal Bible Verses

Many times—more than I can recall—I've gone to my desk in heaviness or distress. I've been anxious or angry or senseless with worry. With a prayer for guidance, I've opened my Bible, often where I left off the day before. Sometimes I've tracked down other verses cross-referenced in the margin. Sometimes I've gone to passages I've known for years; other times I've plunged into sections of Scripture that are less familiar. Always I have found a verse that spoke to my situation, as though the Lord Himself were speaking to me, giving perspective and renewed strength.

Isaiah 30:21 says, "Your ears shall hear a word behind you, saying, 'This is the way, walk in it,' whenever you turn to the right hand, or whenever you turn to the left" (NKJV).

This is God's primary way in helping His people draw near Him. Psalm 119:151 says, "You are near, LORD, and all your commands are true."

In practical terms, that means we need to know how to find Bible verses so we can put our names in them, as Marie Monsen did with Isaiah 41:10. Studying the Bible isn't merely an academic exercise; it's a personal relationship. God speaks to us through the personalization of Scripture.

But we must do this wisely, following the instructions of 2 Timothy 2:15: "Present yourself to God as one approved, a worker who does not need to be ashamed and who correctly handles the word of truth." Finding and applying God's Word requires the careful handling and diligent study of Scripture, but there is no richer pursuit.

Here are four simple ways to find your own personal verses in the Bible.

> Studying the Bible isn't merely an academic exercise; it's a personal relationship.

First, mark verses that speak to you. Read the Bible each day, starting where you left off the day before. It's best to have a method to your Bible reading. I enjoy tackling a book at a time, like Psalms or Philippians. Suppose you choose the book of Philippians, one of my favorites. If you own a study Bible containing background material, read the introductory comments. Then start with chapter 1, verse 1, and, asking God to guide you, pore over each verse in order. Ponder each word.

> Paul and Timothy, servants of Christ Jesus, to all God's holy people in Christ Jesus at Philippi, together with the overseers and deacons: Grace and peace to you from God our Father and the Lord Jesus Christ. I thank my God every time I remember you. In all my prayers for all of you, I always pray with joy. (vv. 1–4)

You may get no further the first day, for there is much here to consider. Maybe the word *servants* spoke to you. Am I a servant of Christ? What does that look like? What does that say about my attitude today?

Perhaps you lingered on the words *grace and peace*—qualities you need right now.

For me, it was the part about praying with joy that stood out in my reading. Usually I pray for someone because I'm worried about that person, and sometimes my worries spiral downward as I pray. But what about infusing our prayers with joy?

Going on, you read:

> I always pray with joy because of your partnership in the gospel from the first day until now, being confident of this, that he who began a good work in you will carry it on to completion until the day of Christ Jesus. (vv. 4–6)

What a promise! God is not finished with us yet. He has started a good work in us, but we're still under construction. He'll keep working on us till Christ returns.

Second, memorize verses that speak to you. As you find a verse such as Philippians 1:6, you may want to memorize it. Write it on a card and read it aloud several times a day:

> He who began a good work in you will carry it on to completion until the day of Christ Jesus. (Philippians 1:6)

When you memorize a verse, it's with you forever, and its truth sinks deeply into your spirit. Proverbs 7:1–3 tells us to store up God's commands within us and write them on the tablets of our hearts. I began doing this in childhood through Bible memory programs at school and church. In recent years I've rededicated myself to working each day on a passage of Scripture. Currently I'm learning Psalm 113, which contains this wonderful image of God: "Who is like the LORD our God, the One who sits enthroned on high, who stoops down to look on the heavens and the earth?" (vv. 5–6).

As you learn a verse by heart, keep a record of it and review it. As time goes by, your assortment of memorized verses will become your most valuable collectibles.

Third, meditate on Bible verses that speak to you. When you've memorized a portion of Scripture, you can turn it into a portable Bible study wherever you go. Of course, you don't have to memorize a verse to contemplate it. With your Bible open to Philippians, you can read, ponder, and personalize each verse as you come to it. But some verses are worth learning, for then you can meditate on them day and night.

In *Reclaiming the Lost Art of Biblical Meditation*, I wrote, "Like water flowing through a fountain or oil through a machine, Scripture should be constantly circulating through our minds so that we become God-conditioned. In the process, we start to look at things as He does, which is the essence of wisdom."[1]

Joshua 1:8–9 says, "Meditate on [Scripture] day and night. . . .

Do not be afraid; do not be discouraged, for the LORD your God will be with you wherever you go." In other words, when we ponder the Scriptures day and night, we experience God's nearness all the time. If someone follows you everywhere, whispering in your ear all day, you're aware of his presence. When you meditate on Scripture, it's as though the Holy Spirit is following you, whispering in your ear. He brings verses to mind day and night, often in times of fear or frustration. No practice in life has helped me more than Scripture memory and biblical meditation.

When you meditate on Scripture, it's as though the Holy Spirit is following you, whispering in your ear.

Finally, we must make those verses our own through faith and obedience. For a stronger faith, focus your mental energy on the verses God gives you. That's the best exercise of the soul. Where there is a command, obey it. Where there is a prayer, offer it. Where there is a truth, believe it. Where there is a message, repeat it. Where there is a promise, claim it by faith.

Last year I took my grandson, Elijah, hiking. At one point the trail wound along a steep embankment. Elijah scampered up like a deer, but I had trouble. Fortunately, the engineers had installed eyebolts into the stone and had run a thick, knotted rope through them. By grabbing the knots in the rope, I ascended the mountainside more easily.

The knotted rope of God's promises runs through the length of the Bible, attached by the eyebolts of His watchful concern and bolted into the rock of His unchanging faithfulness. Find your own Bible verses. Mark them. Memorize some of them. Meditate on them day and night, and make them your own through faith and obedience.

> When quiet in my house I sit,
> Thy Book be my companion still,
> My joy Thy sayings to repeat,
> Talk o'er the records of Thy will,
> And search the oracles divine,
> Till every heartfelt word be mine.
>
> CHARLES WESLEY, "WHEN QUIET IN MY HOUSE I SIT"

Reading the Whole Bible Every Day

I wish I could read the whole Bible every day—all 1,189 chapters. There aren't enough hours in the day for that, yet I need the whole range of Scripture to bear me through each day.

In the morning, seeing the rising sun from my upstairs window, I need to remember Genesis 1:1: "In the beginning God created the heavens and the earth." When I watch the news about conflicts in the Middle East, I need to recall God's promises to Abraham in Genesis 12. When things go wrong in my day, it's helpful to recall what Joseph said in Genesis 50:20: "You intended to harm me, but God intended it for good to accomplish what is now being done."

As I plunge into my work, I should let the Ten Commandments

in Exodus 20 govern my behavior. And how useful to meet everyone today in the spirit of Leviticus 19:18: "Love your neighbor as yourself." The book of Numbers reminds me to serve God without muttering and complaining. And I need Deuteronomy to remind me, "The eternal God is your refuge, and underneath are the everlasting arms" (33:27).

The book of Joshua begins, "I will never leave you nor forsake you. Be strong and courageous" (1:5–6). Judges warns against doing what is right in my own eyes without regard for God. As the little book of Ruth reminds me, even in turbulent times God brings love and laughter into each day.

When I face Goliaths in my pathway, it's helpful to remember what the boy David said, slingshot in hand, "The battle is the LORD's" (1 Samuel 17:47). Speaking of David, his words in Psalm 55:22 tell me what to do when the load becomes heavy: "Cast your cares on the LORD, and he will sustain you; he will never let the righteous be shaken."

A day shouldn't pass without the exuberance of Psalm 100: "Shout for joy to the LORD, all the earth. Worship the LORD with gladness; come before him with joyful songs" (vv. 1–2).

The afternoon is a good time to read Proverbs, with its advice on integrity, cheerfulness, and dependability.

I need Isaiah to keep me strong; Jeremiah to keep me tender;

Ezekiel to keep me looking to the future; and Daniel to remind me the Most High rules over human affairs.

Even the Minor Prophets are worth reading every afternoon. Hosea reminds me to love the wife God gave me; Jonah tells me to go wherever God sends; and Habakkuk shows me to trust God when the fig tree doesn't bud and there are no grapes on the vine.

As the day wanes and my work is only half done, how important to remember what Jesus said in Matthew's gospel: "Seek first [God's] kingdom and his righteousness, and all these things will be given to you as well" (6:33).

And in Mark's gospel: "Whoever wants to be my disciple must deny themselves and take up their cross and follow me" (8:34).

In Luke's: "Consider the ravens: They do not sow or reap, they have no storeroom or barn; yet God feeds them. And how much more valuable you are than birds!" (12:24).

I need Isaiah to keep me strong; Jeremiah to keep me tender; Ezekiel to keep me looking to the future; and Daniel to remind me the Most High rules over human affairs.

And these words in John's gospel: "Do not let your hearts be troubled. You believe in God; believe also in me" (14:1).

Never a day without thinking of our Lord's cross and His empty tomb! Never a day without the power of the Holy Spirit, which descended in the book of Acts and filled the believers so they spoke the gospel with boldness (Acts 4:31).

Every evening I need Romans 12:11: "Never be lacking in zeal, but keep your spiritual fervor, serving the Lord." When unwinding, I need a dose of Philippians 4:5–6: "The Lord is near. Do not be anxious about anything, but in every situation, by prayer and petition, with thanksgiving, present your requests to God."

I can tuck myself into bed with Hebrews 4:16: "Let us then approach God's throne of grace with confidence, so that we may receive mercy and find grace to help us in our time of need."

I need all the Bible every day.

As I click off the bedside light, I need to remember the book of Revelation and its vivid descriptions of the future and heaven. Should I awaken during the night, I can recall the final promise in the Bible and whisper its concluding prayer: "He who testifies to these things says, 'Yes, I am coming soon.' Amen. Come, Lord Jesus" (Revelation 22:20).

You see, I need *all* the Bible *every* day.

42

But since I can't read the whole Bible daily, I must at least read a portion of it each day, learn some of its verses, and ask the Holy Spirit to bring them to mind as needed.

And you? Since you can't read the whole Bible every day, read a book of the Bible. If you can't read a book, read a chapter. If you can't read a chapter, read a verse. And if you can't read a verse, well, rearrange your schedule.

Take time to be still and know that He is God.

> *O that Thy statutes every hour*
> *Might dwell upon my mind!*
> *Thence I derive a quickening power*
> *And daily peace I find.*
> Isaac Watts, "O That Thy Statutes"

delight

in Speaking
to God

Praying in Deep Water

Years ago, I found a quote that changed how I viewed prayer: "[The] chief purpose of prayer [is] to realize the presence of your heavenly Father."[1]

Deuteronomy 4:7 agrees: "What other nation is so great as to have their gods near them the way the LORD our God is near us whenever we pray to him?"

The Lord our God is near to us whenever we pray to Him. The Creator of the cosmos bends His ear to our praises, listens to our pleas, and pauses to hear each need. Psalm 145:18 says, "The LORD is near to all who call on him, to all who call on him in truth."

Jeremiah said, "You came near when I called you, and you said, 'Do not fear'" (Lamentations 3:57).

Jesus spoke of prayer as a deliberate and regular habit: "When you pray, go into your room, close the door and pray to your Father, who is unseen. Then your Father, who sees what is done in secret, will reward you" (Matthew 6:6).

Your "room" may be anywhere. Just ask Jonah.

Recently I studied the book of Jonah and tried to imagine how Jonah felt as he flew overboard into the Mediterranean Sea. The shock of cold. The water soaking his robes and pulling him downward. The stinging salt. The sense of drowning. The ominous shadow of a sea creature. The sensation of being swallowed alive. The slime and mucus. The claustrophobia and seaweed and smell.

How would you have felt? What would you have done for the next three days?

Jonah could have screamed incessantly. He could have raged. He could have kicked the fish in the ribs and beaten his fists against its stomach. He could have tried to escape, struggling to crawl out the way he came in. He might have sunk in self-pity and depression, or worried himself to death, or languished in boredom, or given up, or composed an essay on the anatomy of big fish. Maybe he did a little of all those things, but we're only told of one thing he did: "Jonah was in the belly of the fish three days and three nights. From inside the fish Jonah *prayed*" (Jonah 1:17–2:1; emphasis added).

He prayed earnestly and intelligently. Though Jonah was entombed beneath tons of water, his prayer flew to the highest heaven, unfettered, unhindered—and it changed Jonah, it changed Nineveh, and it changed history. More precisely, God was with Jonah there in the fish, showing him that prayer isn't the last resort; it's the best option.

For Jonah, the fish's stomach became a communications center unrivaled by the most advanced submarine. That speaks to me. I've never been swallowed by a giant fish, but I've been inside a lot of problems that made me want to scream, rage, worry, despair, languish, overanalyze, or give up.

But Jonah turned his panic into prayer and his prayer into praise. It calmed his spirits and restored his mind. He drew closer to God in the sea than he had been on land. Jonah said, "In my distress I called to the LORD, and he answered me. From deep in the realm of the dead I called for help, and you listened to my cry" (Jonah 2:2).

God was with Jonah there in the fish, showing him that prayer isn't the last resort; it's the best option.

The longer Jonah prayed, the better he felt—and the sicker the fish became, finally spitting him onto dry ground. And that's what prayer does—it thrills the Lord, nauseates the devil, and frees us. Our problems simply cannot imprison us when we pray. Without prayer, we're trapped by the troubles of life; when we pray, God turns those troubles into tools for accomplishing His will. Prayer invites God into our space, and when He comes in, He takes over.

Eliza and Abram Garfield were married in 1820. One day the fields around their cabin caught fire, and Abram lost his life while fighting the inferno. Eliza, a woman of strong faith, determined to raise their children alone.

Her son, James, was a handful—driven, determined, and precocious. Against his mother's wishes, he left home at sixteen to work on the Ohio and Erie Canal.

One rainy night about midnight, James was alone on the bow of the ship. He picked up a coil of loose rope and lost his balance, falling headlong over the railing into black waters, just like Jonah. The other sailors were below deck, unable to hear his cries.

The water was dark and deep, and there seemed no way to

> Prayer invites God into our space, and when He comes in, He takes over.

survive. James cried out in prayer. Suddenly, his hand felt the untethered rope. As he grabbed it in desperation, it snagged on something.

James pulled himself, hand over hand, onto the deck and collapsed, chilled and terrified, wondering what had saved him. He discovered that as the rope had zipped along the railing, its end had caught in a crevice. He realized God had a plan for his life, and he resolved to go home.

It was a long journey, and he battled high fever, arriving home almost too weak to walk. As he staggered toward the cabin, he saw a light in the window. Peering in, he saw his mother kneeling in the corner, a book open before her, her eyes lifted toward heaven. She was praying for him.

For weeks, Eliza nursed her son back to health. He later enrolled in a Freewill Baptist school and shortly afterward trusted Christ as his Savior. He began preaching and later became the only president of the United States who was also an ordained minister. Eliza was the first mother to watch her son take the oath of office as commander in chief,[2] and all because Eliza knew how to take her burdens to the Lord.

Prayer isn't a matter of sending words billions of miles into space toward an unseen power. It's simply talking to a Friend who comes to join you in your room, whether it's by a cabin hearth or inside a fish's belly. Prayer is recognizing the presence of the heavenly Father and casting your cares on Him.

Are you in deep water? Deep sorrow? Deep anxiety? Deep trouble? David wrote, "He reached down from on high and took hold of me; he drew me out of deep waters" (Psalm 18:16). There are no depths like the fathomless billows of God's love. So, when you come to the end of your rope, don't sink in despair. Find a knot, hang on, and draw near to God in prayer.

What If God Says No?

The Bible is a prayer book. Every chapter and verse can be converted to prayer, and our most effective prayers are those forged from Scripture. Using Psalm 23:6 for an example, you might pray, "Lord, may goodness and mercy follow me all the days of my life, and may I dwell in Your house forever."

The Bible also contains the world's most powerful data about prayer, and three verses are favorites of mine:

- "Jesus told his disciples a parable to show them that they should always pray and not give up." (Luke 18:1)

- "The prayer of a righteous person is powerful and effective." (James 5:16)
- "This is the confidence we have in approaching God: that if we ask anything according to his will, he hears us. And if we know that he hears us—whatever we ask—we know that we have what we asked of him." (1 John 5:14–15)

Prayer is a conversation with God whereby we draw near to Him and ascertain His will for life. Since we cannot see the future, we don't know the best route, so we pray as best we can, in the name of Jesus, then say, "Lord, if it be Your will." God always answers our prayers. Often He says yes.

But sometimes God says no.

When my grandson, Elijah, was five, he started throwing up around bedtime. He came to his parents' room in tears, begging for prayer. They held him close and prayed, and he went back to bed. A few minutes later, he was back, holding a pail and crying, "It didn't work! Praying didn't work!"

"So we curled up in bed and had a little talk about it," his mom later told me.

Sometimes prayer doesn't seem to work, and we need to discuss that with the Father. When faced with some answers of no in my own experiences, I gained strength by looking at times

God said no to biblical heroes and studying how that worked out for them.

- In Genesis 17:18, Abraham prayed, "If only Ishmael might live under your blessing!" God had promised Abraham that He would make him the "father of many nations. . . . Kings will come from you," He said (vv. 4, 6). Abraham, despairing of a son, asked God to fulfill His promise through Ishmael, his son through a servant. But God had a better plan. One year later, Isaac, whose family line would one day produce the Messiah, was born to Abraham and his wife, Sarah, in their old age.

- In Deuteronomy 3:23–25, Moses pleaded for the privilege of leading the Israelites into the promised land. God said no. Moses died on the heights of Pisgah, and Joshua led the Israelites into the land. But later Moses set foot in Israel alongside Christ Himself on the Mount of Transfiguration. The *no* was the doorway to a bigger *yes* in God's timing.

- In 1 Chronicles 17, King David prayed about building a temple for the Lord in Jerusalem, but God said no. That job was Solomon's, but God also told David of a coming king whose throne would be established forever—a promise fulfilled by Jesus Christ, Son of David.

- In 1 Kings 19:4, the prophet Elijah, exhausted, prayed to die. "I have had enough, LORD," he said. "Take my life." God said no—and such a resounding *no* that Elijah *never* died. God snatched him up to heaven in a chariot of fire (v. 11).
- In Mark 5:18, Jesus cast demons out of a man who then begged to become one of His disciples. "Jesus did not let him, but said, 'Go home to your own people and tell them how much the Lord has done for you, and how he has had mercy on you.' So the man went away and began to tell in the Decapolis how much Jesus had done for him. And all the people were amazed" (vv. 19–20).
- In 2 Corinthians 12:8, Paul wrote of praying earnestly on three occasions for healing from an unnamed affliction. God said no, adding, "My grace is sufficient for you, for my power is made perfect in weakness" (v. 9). Somehow Paul was more useful with his affliction than without it.
- In Luke 22:42, Jesus prayed in Gethsemane, "Father, if you are willing, take this cup from me; yet not my will, but yours be done." The greatest unanswered prayer in the Bible was heaven's silence to that plaintive cry, yet our Lord's death and resurrection provided access to God, making it possible for us to draw near Him in abiding, eternal friendship.

When God says no to our urgent pleas, it's because a bigger *yes* is coming. This isn't easy to learn; it requires a walk of faith. But God's timing always turns His vetoes into our victories.

When I finished school in 1976, I returned to Tennessee, expecting to pastor a church. Since Katrina and I were planning our wedding, I wanted to hurry and find a place of ministry and employment. But no churches were interested in me.

Our wedding in Maine was followed by uncertainty about where to live and work. I got two jobs—at Sears and at JCPenney—and Katrina worked in a discount store. I preached for anyone who would have me.

By our count, we visited a dozen churches needing pastors. Many of these were small and couldn't provide much salary or opportunity, yet we hoped they would call us. One day a very good church expressed interest, and we got our hopes up. When they turned us down, I faced a level of discouragement I'd never known.

Meanwhile, our first baby was born, and we had no insurance, little income, no house of our own, and zero prospects for employment. Over and over, the Lord had said no.

> When God says no to our urgent pleas, it's because a bigger *yes* is coming.

Then, just like that, the door opened. On our first wedding anniversary, we began pastoring Harris Memorial Church in Greeneville, Tennessee. That paved the way for forty-one years of pastoral work in two great churches, and I wouldn't have missed the trip for anything.

Only later did my friend Bob Thomas tell me he had prayed that I wouldn't begin pastoring until Katrina and I had been married a full year. He'd been impressed by Deuteronomy 24:5, which says, "If a man has recently married, he must not be sent to war or have any other duty laid on him. For one year he is to be free to stay at home and bring happiness to the wife he has married."

The Lord said yes to Bob's prayers, and no to mine, and I praise Him for that now. Where I was once confused, I've grown thankful. The Lord gave us a year to grow our marriage, and He spared us from several less-than-ideal situations while preparing the opportunity He had planned for us all along.

God's no is better than anyone else's yes. The One who knows the end from the beginning understands the route. We must draw near to Him and trust. We should always pray and not lose heart.

> *They who seek the throne of grace*
> *Find that throne in every place;*
> *If we live a life of prayer,*

God is present everywhere.
In our sickness and our health,
In our want, or in our wealth,
If we look to God in prayer,
God is present everywhere.

OLIVER HOLDEN, "THEY WHO SEEK THE THRONE OF GRACE"

The Needed Calm

No two marriages are alike. The same is true of friendships, including friendship with God. We each have our own way of enjoying God. We bring our individual personalities and backgrounds into the mix, and we develop unique patterns for approaching God in prayer. Just as no two cooks stir the pot the same way, your manner of praying is likely very different from mine.

Still, it has helped me immensely to discover how other people pray, and by talking to them or reading their books, I've picked up useful hints. My own plan involves a notebook, a zippered binder with half-size paper. One section is a journal, where each morning I spend a few minutes jotting down what's going on in my life. If I'm troubled, I write more. Then I turn to my Bible and start reading where I left off the day before, looking for some insight, verse, promise, prayer, command, or reassurance. When I find it, I jot it down. In this way I listen as God speaks.

The second part of my notebook is for prayer and contains several pages. Working through them, I often pray aloud. Many Christians only pray silently, but I often prefer to speak to God as if speaking to a friend at hand.

> Many Christians only pray silently, but I often prefer to speak to God as if speaking to a friend at hand.

The first page in my prayer section says, "Thanksgiving," and each morning I think of something new for which to give thanks. I write it down and praise God for it.

The next page says, "Daily Prayers," and there I've penned some Bible verses to pray into my life every day, such as 1 Chronicles 4:10: "Oh, that You would bless me indeed and enlarge my territory. Let Your hand be with me and keep me from evil, that I might not cause pain" (paraphrased). Also on this page are names of people I pray for daily, including family members. Other pages say "Missionaries" and "Prodigals." Another page shows a map of the world, and I pray for specific nations and missionaries each day. I also pray for our leaders.

The remainder of the pages contain a running list of burdens or opportunities arranged by month. Last month my list contained forty numbered items. When the Lord answers one of my requests, I thank Him and circle the number. When I thumb through the pages, I note the unanswered items and continue to mention them to the Lord. As I work through my lists, I speak to God face-to-face, as it were, in the name of Christ.

I end my time with the Lord by asking Him what to do today. Glancing at my calendar and to-do lists, I plan my day. Sometimes I read from a devotional book or sing from a hymnbook. Singing, to me, is critical to drawing near to God. I'm not a vocalist, but alone in my room, I often feel close to God while singing a great hymn, such as "Praise to the Lord, the Almighty." Apart from the Bible, the hymnal offers our greatest treasure trove of devotional truth and spiritual nourishment.

How long does all this take? About thirty minutes, more or less (usually a bit more). All this may seem overwhelming to you, but you can develop your own system to fit your personality and schedule. Don't pray as I do. Find your own patterns. Your prayer time might involve

- a morning prayer walk through your neighborhood
- resting in bed upon waking, praying as the sun filters through the windows
- donning headphones and praying silently on your train ride to work
- talking to God amid rush-hour traffic on your commute home
- soaking in the hot tub and talking to the Lord at the close of day
- kneeling at your bedside to pray before falling asleep
- rocking in your favorite chair as you pray

Our regular daily prayer time isn't the totality of our communication with God; it simply sets the stage for it. The Bible tells us to pray continually (1 Thessalonians 5:17). When you leave your room in the morning, the Lord goes with you. Frequently throughout the day, learn to say, "Thank You, Lord," or, "Help me, Lord," or, "Bless them, Lord," or, "Give me patience!" While preparing for bedtime, thank the Lord for the mercies of the day. But don't forget to have a habitual daily time when you're quiet long enough to sense His presence. Without spaces of sacred stillness, we'll unravel like a cheap sweater. It's difficult to delight in the closeness of God while neglecting the needed calm of daily conversation with Him through prayer and the study of the Word. His nearness brings His peace, for that's what we read in one of the Bible's greatest promises:

> The Lord is near. Do not be anxious about anything, but in every situation, by prayer and petition, with thanksgiving, present your requests to God. And the peace of God, which transcends all understanding, will guard your hearts and your minds in Christ Jesus.
>
> PHILIPPIANS 4:5–7

delight

in the
Splendor of
Worship

How Christ Came to Church

The Bible says that God inhabits the praises of His people. Well, actually, it doesn't. No verse in the Bible contains those oft-quoted words. But three verses convey similar meaning:

- "But thou art holy, O thou that inhabitest the praises of Israel." (Psalm 22:3 KJV)
- "God is present in the company of the righteous." (Psalm 14:5)
- "Where two or three gather in my name, there am I with them." (Matthew 18:20)

We draw close to God in a unique way when we join other believers, just as a family builds memories and accrues love while gathering at the old home place. We need the kind of closeness engendered by family gatherings, which means—for God's people—the church.

After fulfilling His earthly ministry, Christ ascended heavenward to His rightful place on the throne of God. He didn't leave behind any universities. He didn't establish political parties or military operations. He didn't even found benevolent organizations. But He said, "I will build My church" (Matthew 16:18 NKJV).

For two thousand years, Jesus has been working on earth by His Spirit through local churches, some large, some small, scattered around the world. Out of these churches have come the universities, the benevolent organizations, the missionary enterprises, and the societal reforms that have changed history. When we attend church each week, we are drawing near to God by drawing close to the people indwelt by His Spirit. He is present in the company of the righteous.

Boston pastor A. J. Gordon described a dream he had one Saturday night after he had gone to bed weary from preparing the next morning's sermon.

I was in the pulpit ready to begin my sermon when a stranger entered and passed up the aisle of the church looking first to one side and then to the other. He proceeded nearly halfway up the aisle when a gentleman offered him a place in his pew, which was quietly accepted. Immediately as I began my sermon my attention became riveted on this hearer. If I would avert my eyes from him for a moment they would instinctively return to him, so that he held my attention rather than I held his till the discourse was ended.

To myself I constantly said, "Who can that stranger be?" and mentally resolved to find out. But after the benediction, the departing congregation filed into the aisles and before I could reach him the visitor had left. The gentleman with whom he had sat remained behind; and approaching him with eagerness I asked, "Can you tell me who that stranger was in your pew this morning?"

In the most matter-of-course way he replied, "Why, do you not know that man? It was Jesus of Nazareth."[1]

Dr. Gordon awoke with a start and realized Christ was the unseen Presence in every gathering of His people. Gordon immediately began thinking about the relationship between Christ and the Holy Spirit. On the eve of His crucifixion, Jesus told His followers He was returning to heaven. He said, "I will ask the Father, and he will give you another advocate [literally, someone to come alongside you] to help you and be with you forever—the Spirit of truth. . . . You know him, for he lives with you and will be in you. I will not leave you as orphans" (John 14:16–18).

"As truly as Christ went up, the Holy Ghost came down," said Gordon in his book *How Christ Came to Church.* "The one took his place at the Father's right hand in heaven, the other took his seat in the church on earth. . . . The Lord himself is truly though invisibly here in the midst of every company of disciples gathered in any place in His name."[2]

How incredible to consider! No matter how frustrated we get with our churches—and believe me, as a pastor I've gotten as frustrated as anyone—the Lord Jesus is at every gathering through the presence of the Holy Spirit as actually as He once stood in the Upper Room. He is there as we sing. He is there as we preach. He is there as we greet one another, pray together, and bear one another's burdens. He is there as we break the bread and taste the

> We are dangerously close to considering the church dispensable. It isn't.

wine and baptize the converts. He is there as we praise His name and extend the gospel.

Our culture is becoming less interested in church, and thus, further detached from the presence of Christ. We are dangerously close to considering the church dispensable. It isn't. The Bible commands God's people to assemble together, "and all the more as you see the Day approaching" (Hebrews 10:25).

If Jesus comes to church, should I be so frequently absent?

Why do I go to church? Not because the people are perfect, the music beautiful, the sermons entertaining, the programming relevant, the location convenient, or the style to my liking. I attend church to draw nearer to Jesus, for He is present among His gathered children. He truly does inhabit the praises of His people.

Revival

In *Worry Less, Live More*, I wrote about my friend Hester Rendall, who lived on the Hebrides island of Lewis. A revival had swept the island between 1949 and 1952, and though Hester didn't arrive until 1958, the afterglow was still evident. One evening in church a sense of God's presence descended so strongly that the people prayed earnestly and hardly dared lift their heads. Eventually, Hester's friend leaned over and suggested they leave. "Why?" Hester said. "We've only been here a few minutes."

The friend answered, "It's three o'clock in the morning."[1]

Those who study revivals come across many stories in which the presence of God sweeps so intensely through a geographical zone that people are awed and brought to instant conviction and conversion. Wesley Duewel wrote of the 1857 revival in America,

"The presence of the Holy Spirit . . . seemed to hang like an invisible cloud over many parts of the United States, especially over the eastern seaboard. At times this cloud of God's presence even seemed to extend out to sea. Those on ships approaching the east coast at times felt a solemn, holy influence, even one hundred miles away."[2]

As a student at Wheaton College, I recall hearing of the revival that gripped the campus in February 1950, when Dr. Raymond Edman was the school's president. In his account, Edman wrote of the "sense of awe and reverence because of the immediacy of God in our midst."[3]

Some students were working off campus at the time, yet as they crossed the property line of the college, a sense of the presence of God came over them. One man, Paul Holsinger, was driving to the university's academy the next morning. He knew nothing of the revival, but as he drove along Highway 64 toward the school, "his own heart was so overwhelmed with the sense of God's presence that he drove to the side of the road and stopped for prayer. Later he told us that he remained sometime there in prayer with tears as he worshipped the Lord in the true beauty of holiness."[4]

The only hope for our society is another revival, unleashed by the Holy Spirit, to fill our churches and homes with an overwhelmingly tangible sense of the presence of God in the beauty of His holiness. We can prepare for revival by prayer, repentance, and renewed commitment, yet we cannot orchestrate or implement supernatural awakenings. That's the work of the Holy Spirit. Our job is to live in His presence even if it isn't manifested as dramatically as during periodic revivals. Our society may or may not experience the kind of widespread awakening we read about in the Bible and in history, but the Lord longs to keep us personally revived with the daily enthusiasm of His presence.

> The only hope for our society is another revival, unleashed by the Holy Spirit.

In his final words to Timothy, Paul wrote, "In the presence of God and of Christ Jesus, who will judge the living and the dead, and in view of his appearing and his kingdom, I give you this charge: Preach the word" (2 Timothy 4:1–2). This wasn't necessarily a time of supernatural revival. Paul wasn't in chapel; he was chained in prison. Timothy had his hands full with problems in the church in Ephesus. But the apostle said, in effect, "God is near me as I am writing these words to you; and He is present with you as you are reading them; so, in the presence of God and of Christ Jesus, here is my challenge to you—preach the Word."

Revival is living with an awareness of God around us, above us, beside us, and within us. Worship is filling our minds with thoughts of God, our hearts with love for God, and our mouths with praise to God.

When true revival sweeps over our land, we'll enjoy a vivid sense of His presence, but even when revival is not stirring, we are still living in the presence of God and Jesus Christ every day. He dwells among us by the Holy Spirit, and He sits enthroned above the praises of His church. He has promised to be with us.

Do you need a personal revival of God's presence? I do, continually, and it's constantly available.

One morning I awoke with a heavy heart. Coffee didn't help, and not even my Bible reading or prayer time lifted my spirits. But then an old hymn came to mind, and its prayerful words have revived my spirits ever since:

> *I need Thee every hour,*
> *Most gracious Lord;*
> *No tender voice like Thine*
> *Can peace afford.*
> *I need Thee, O, I need Thee;*

Every hour I need Thee;
O, bless me now, my Savior!
I come to Thee.

ANNIE S. HAWKS, "I NEED THEE EVERY HOUR"

delight

in Special Times

Breaks for Inner Refreshment

After the exodus, as the Israelites zigzagged through the desert, the Lord gave them laws to regulate their society (Exodus 20). He enabled Moses to set up a system of government, including a judiciary (Exodus 18) and an army (Numbers 1). He established the spiritual life of the people around the tabernacle (Exodus 40), with priests fulfilling their assigned tasks (Exodus 29). But God did something more. In Leviticus 23, He gave the Israelites an annual calendar, and He blocked out holy days (holidays) for them, a set of festivals for physical and spiritual renewal. In other words, He invented the first vacations.

At the heart of the system was a weekly Sabbath for rest and worship. The schedule also included the Passover; the Festivals of Unleavened Bread, Firstfruits, Weeks, Trumpets (or Ingathering), and Tabernacles; and the Day of Atonement. The Festival of Tabernacles, something of an annual national camping trip, was especially festive. Around campfires, parents told their children the great things God had done and instilled in their hearts a love for the abiding presence of the Lord throughout the pilgrimage of life.

Many of these celebrations involved special food, and some involved traveling. Three times a year Jewish families headed to Jerusalem for celebrations at the temple. Some of the psalms were written for pilgrims to sing as they crossed mountains and valleys while traveling to Zion for joyful worship. These were seasons of refreshment, built around a God-given calendar with regular times for the Jewish people to draw closer to Him.

How badly we need such a calendar! How important to build time into our schedules for drawing nearer to God and regulating the pace of life. When we operate full throttle, we begin breaking down. We need our daily quiet time. We also need a sacred seventh day each week to counterbalance the pressures of the other six. Neglecting a weekly day of rest weakens us.

We also need longer breaks from time to time. My family loves traveling, but we don't want to leave the Lord behind. As the Israelites learned from the column of fire and smoke over the tabernacle, God is a delightful traveling companion. His presence doesn't preclude fun or rest; it enables them.

Some people drive furiously to a vacation spot, wear themselves out for five days, then race home to be at work the next morning. That's a trip, but not a vacation. We simply must find ways of resting a few days, having fun while still replenishing our hearts with God's nearness.

Here's what I propose: Plan a little trip. Before leaving home, select an inspiring book to read while you're away; find some sermons or uplifting music to listen to on the journey; choose a portion of Scripture to study; and plan your trip so your daily time with the Lord is lengthened a bit, not abbreviated.

How important to build time into our schedules for drawing nearer to God and regulating the pace of life.

If you have children, this may be harder, but the Israelites used their holidays to instill faith in their children. Exodus 12:26–27 says of the Passover, "And when your children ask you, 'What does this ceremony mean to you?' then tell them."

My favorite trips involve a balcony or beach where I can read, study, and think; with a museum or interesting site nearby; some opportunities for exercise, swimming, or hiking; alfresco meals at sidewalk cafés; and lots of rest. I don't have to spend a lot of money for those things. It just takes intentional planning to leverage getaways for renewal. Ask yourself: How can I plan my vacation so I feel closer to God when I return than when I left? How can I find inner rest? How can I design a family trip that brings us closer without wearing us out?

That's the kind of vacation God designed in Leviticus 23.

Occasionally we also need personal retreats, just a day or even a morning. Once, I was handed a problem that seemed unsolvable. I canceled my schedule, drove to a park, and checked in to the inn. For twenty-four hours I read my Bible, prayed, slept, and hiked the lakeside trails, considering my dilemma from every angle. The next afternoon I returned home knowing what should be done.

Our pressures have never been greater, and the pace of life is accelerating like a boulder tumbling downhill. We can't maintain physical health, mental sanity, or spiritual well-being without some blessed breaks. In Mark 6:31, Jesus told His exhausted disciples, "Come with me by yourselves to a quiet place and get some rest." Try personalizing that verse, because you need rest too.

Build seasons of refreshment into your schedule before you

wear yourself out. Just as Jesus withdrew to the wilderness to be with His Father, use your strategic breaks to boost your closeness to Him. Otherwise, your lack of downtime will be your downfall. We need to come apart with the Lord before we come apart at the seams. If we don't unwind, we'll unravel. But if we draw near to God, He will draw near to us, and His nearness will be rejuvenating.

The Invisible Man

Our lives don't stay the same. They are always moving forward, from stage to stage. Every new page is an arena for God's blessing. This came to me forcefully as I read Numbers 33:1–2:

> Here are the stages in the journey of the Israelites when they came out of Egypt by divisions under the leadership of Moses and Aaron. At the LORD's command Moses recorded the stages in their journey. This is their journey by stages.

Three times we're told God led the Israelites by stages. The remainder of the chapter contains a chronological listing of the travels of the children of Israel as they made their way from Egypt to the promised land. Each stage was different, but all the stages had one thing in common—the Lord was with Israel. He dwelled among them as an effervescent cloud by day and a column of fire at night. His presence was constantly manifested. Numbers 9 describes His abiding presence:

> From evening till morning the cloud above the tabernacle looked like fire. That is how it continued to be; the cloud covered it, and at night it looked like fire. Whenever the cloud lifted from above the tent, the Israelites set out; wherever the cloud settled, the Israelites encamped. . . . As long as the cloud stayed over the tabernacle, they remained in camp. When the cloud remained over the tabernacle a long time, the Israelites obeyed the LORD's order and did not set out. Sometimes the cloud was over the tabernacle only a few days; at the LORD's command they would encamp, and then at His command they would set out. Sometimes the cloud stayed only from evening till morning, and when it lifted in the morning, they set out. Whether by day or by night, whenever the cloud lifted, they set out. (vv. 15–21)

Just as God was literally present with the Israelites, guiding them through the desert, He is with you through the stages of your life. Think of Him as a column of cloud by day and a pillar of fire by night, all around you, upon you, within you. When you encounter a rugged stage, He will go to great lengths to help you.

Recently a friend gave me the book *Warriors of Ethiopia*, about local evangelists in Ethiopia who helped spread the gospel through their land. One story involved a man named Nana, who, along with forty-one companions, decided to bring Christ to the province of Gofa. The forty-two men moved into the area, built thatched houses, and began sharing Jesus. Churches sprang up, and the fabric of society began changing.

Enemies of the gospel arose, and the church entered a stage of suffering. The evangelists were seized, along with many new believers. They were whipped and chained. Their houses were burned down; their churches, destroyed. For a while, it looked hopeless.

But one man was not arrested—Nana. Local authorities put a price on his head, yet he was never captured. He didn't run away or hide. He was in the open every day, going about his work. He took care of the forty-one imprisoned evangelists and their families. He delivered food and medicine and encouraged the churches. He was everywhere, but he seemed veiled to the authorities. As Dick McLellan wrote:

Nana was easily identifiable . . . but it seemed he was invisible or the police were blind. When he passed police and officials on the road, they ignored him. At the Bulki prison gate, other visitors waited for permission to enter but Nana walked right past the guards with loads of food. . . . Not once was Nana ever stopped or questioned. The Governor and all his officials could not find Nana, even when he walked in their very presence. The Police Chief, who had his hundreds of soldiers searching for Nana, could not find him, though Nana passed them every day in town and on the country roads.[1]

To this day, Nana is called the Invisible Man. Because of him, Christians were encouraged and the work thrived despite persecution. More than a thousand churches arose in that area, and God was faithful to His suffering people through a difficult stage in the history of the Ethiopian church.[2]

Nana was not actually invisible, of course. Somehow the Lord just kept him from being recognized. It's reminiscent of the story in Luke 24, when the two disciples of Emmaus walked seven miles with Jesus without recognizing Him.

As our lives progress from stage to stage, the Stranger from

> As our lives progress from stage to stage, the Stranger from Galilee walks with us.

Galilee walks with us. We live in His unseen presence, and He knows how to take care of us every step. When you awaken in the morning, He is there. As you prepare for your day, He is near. As you pursue your daily agenda, He hovers beside you. If bad news comes, He hears it. If you grow weak, He can strengthen you. As you turn down the sheets, you can say, "Good night, Lord. Since You're going to stay awake and beside me all night, I'm going to sleep. I entrust myself into Your care."

Jesus is our unseen Friend who walks among us, travels beside us, and leads us through the stages of life. Charlotte Elliott, writer of the beloved hymn "Just as I Am," put it this way in another hymn:

> *O holy Savior, Friend unseen*
> *The faint, the weak on Thee may lean,*
> *Help me, throughout life's varying scene,*
> *By faith to cling to Thee.*
>
> Charlotte Elliott, "O Holy Savior, Friend Unseen"

Embracing God's Presence When He Feels Far Away

"God, who is everywhere, never leaves us," wrote Thomas Merton. "Yet He seems sometimes to be present, sometimes to be absent. If we do not know Him well, we do not realize that He may be more present to us when He is absent than when He is present."[1]

If God doesn't seem near you now, there are two possible reasons. First, maybe some lingering sin is strangling your fellowship with Him. The Bible says, "Do not grieve the Holy Spirit of God, with whom you were sealed for the day of redemption" (Ephesians

4:30). To walk with God, we must avoid things that displease Him, repent of careless behavior, confess evil thoughts, and turn from ungodly habits. "If we claim to have fellowship with him and yet walk in the darkness, we lie and do not live out the truth. But if we walk in the light, as he is in the light, we have fellowship with one another [God and us], and the blood of Jesus, his Son, purifies us from all sin. . . . If we confess our sins, He is faithful and just and will forgive us our sins and purify us from all unrighteousness" (1 John 1:6–9).

After confessing your sin, accept God's full and free forgiveness, and don't live in the shame of it any longer. Put it behind you, for God has already thrown it behind His back (Isaiah 38:17). In other words, "Don't be upset or angry with yourselves any longer because of what you did" (Genesis 45:5 THE VOICE)

But there is a second reason you may not feel close to God right now. As Merton suggested, when God feels absent, He may be more present than ever. He wants you to walk by faith, not by feeling. Spiritual maturity is knowing God is near even when we don't feel His presence.

> Spiritual maturity is knowing God is near even when we don't feel His presence.

Going back to the story in Luke 24, remember those downcast disciples who trudged toward Emmaus? A stranger drew near and questioned them about their melancholy. They walked miles with Him before realizing His identity. Though they weren't aware of it, Jesus Himself was trekking beside them, keeping step, dispelling discouragement. He had risen from the tomb to be near them forever.

Our relationship with Christ is based not on feelings but on faith, which is based on the facts of Scripture. Facts, faith, and feeling—that's God's order of things. If our facts are right, our Christian faith will be sound, and our positive feelings will come in due time.

Recently I talked about this with Randy Posslenzny, who grew up in a troubled Michigan home. His mother was married six times, nearly always to an alcoholic, and Randy, as a youth, got involved with a gang and ultimately started taking drugs. Joining the army, he was stationed in Okinawa, Japan, where a friend invited him to a gospel meeting.

"A young evangelist shared the gospel," said Randy. "I had always compared myself to other people and thought I was pretty good. He invited us to consider a holy God who cannot tolerate sin. For the first time, I got a glimpse of the holiness of God, and I knew I was a sinner. I wept. When I heard the gospel, my tears of remorse became tears of joy. I was very emotional. I asked Christ to come into my life, and the next day I was baptized. My drinking buddies said, 'What did you do that for?' But suddenly my father-less vacuum was filled with a Father who wanted to be with me, who wanted to communicate, who loved me. I fell in love with God and would read and read in the Scriptures.

"For five years," Randy continued, "I had a very strong relationship with God. Then one day in Bible college, the sense of the presence of God vanished. I woke up one morning and had my devotions as always, but it was like the ceiling was brass. My prayers bounced right back.

"I was shaken by this loss of emotion. Until then I really felt God was my friend, with me there in the room or wherever. But that morning something happened. I didn't know what it was. It went on for months. I didn't feel or experience God. I had felt so close to Him, as if He were my best friend, and now it was as though He left me.

"One day in the dorm, I got on my knees and prayed, 'Oh, God, what's happening?' The Lord gave me a verse in Romans, 'The just shall live by faith.' It was as though He were saying, 'Randy, I have taken you by the hand as a child and walked with you for five years, and now I want you to live by faith. I want you to pray to Me when you don't feel like praying. I want you to read your Bible when you don't feel like reading it. I want you to witness when you don't feel like witnessing. I want you to understand what it means to follow Me by faith, not by emotions.'

"That learning curve took several months. But I learned the presence of God is not altered by our feelings. He is there whether we feel Him or not. I learned I could look at God's promises and take Him at His Word, knowing He is close to me, whatever my feelings."[2]

This is the common experience of all who walk by faith.

Jonathan Edwards was the greatest preacher of colonial times. One day his daughter, Esther, wrote him a letter praising God for His nearness during her recent trials. Edwards wrote back, "God will never fail those who trust in Him. But don't be surprised, or think some strange thing has happened to you, if after this light, clouds of darkness should return. Perpetual sunshine is not usual in this world, even to God's true saints."[3]

> "Perpetual sunshine is not usual in this world, even to God's true saints."
> —Jonathan Edwards

We often enjoy the sunshine of God's presence and feel the warmth of His rays on us, but perpetual sunshine isn't typical in this world. Yet even when skies are overcast, the Son still shines and God is near those who walk with Him by faith.

part six

delight

in Special

People

Refreshing People

Choose your friends carefully, implies the Bible, because they will pull you nearer to God or push you away from Him. Psalm 1 says, "Blessed is the one who does not walk in step with the wicked or stand in the way that sinners take or sit in the company of mockers" (v. 1). Proverbs opens similarly: "My son, if sinful men entice you, do not give in to them" (1:10). On the other hand, some people have a way of drawing us closer to God. "Walk with the wise and become wise," says Proverbs 13:20.

When I think of those who helped establish my walk with the Lord, I think of my parents, my pastors, my daughters, and especially my wife, Katrina, who has consistently urged me to trust God instead of faltering.

Last fall, Katrina had emergency surgery while I was out of

town. When I arrived at home, I found her laboring to breathe. We feared her surgery had exacerbated her multiple sclerosis, and we wondered if paralysis was constricting her lungs. The doctors sent her to intensive care, and I was frightened. I was also anxious about another matter. As a professional worrier, I know how to worry about two things at once.

Even through her breathing mask, Katrina could sense my distress, and we gripped hands and prayed. Her earnest prayers came in shallow gasps. I wondered if it was our last prayer together.

Katrina, who knows me better than anyone, prayed in weakness better than I could pray in strength. Together, we committed each other and our cares into our Father's hands.

That evening in intensive care was awful. Worried about my wife, plagued by other fears, unable to sleep, and baffled by beeps and whirling noises, I needed some intensive care too. But the Lord was with us, and Katrina and I bolstered each other all night long. God got us through that difficult stage.

The Lord has sent other mentors across my path, and I thank Him for the friends, sermons, lectures, books, and conversations that have helped me. Let me tell you about one of my most unforgettable mentors.

On Mother's Day weekend in 1972, three of us students were invited to North Carolina to spend the weekend with Ruth

Graham while her husband, Billy, was out of town.[1] Upon our arrival, a smiling face appeared in a window, and Ruth came out to greet us. As she showed us around her house, she told us she had scoured local farms for broken-down barns, salvaged the old logs, and shipped them here to be reassembled into the cabin that became her home. Ruth had filled it with odds and ends from antique stores and salvage shops.

Afterward, we sat on the porch. Beyond the fence was an endless expanse of mountains. Ruth talked about her love for the place, for the Lord, and for Billy.

We asked her about the fame that accompanied her husband's role as "America's Pastor." She told us that Billy never saw any glory to his ministry. It was just hard work. He labored to exhaustion, driven by an overwhelming burden. She and Billy would have been happy as missionaries in an obscure land, she said. Indeed, she had always wanted to be a missionary, but God had called her to be an evangelist's wife. But whatever their profession, she added, God's work requires humility. Psalm 115:1 says, "Not to us, LORD, not to us, but to your name be the glory."

She spoke of her study of Philippians 2:13, which says God works in us to both *will* and *do* His good pleasure. God gives both the impulse and the ability to do His work, she said. The desire as well as the ability come from Him.

Ruth went on to reveal that she and her husband needed frequent replenishment, both physical and spiritual. So they would often take short trips to renew their strength and to allow them to spend some unhindered time with the Lord. Before leaving town, they would choose inspiring sermons and music to listen to as they traveled, and books and scriptures to read that would refresh their spirits, much as I suggested in Part Five. That spring, while they were resting in Florida, Billy was having some health issues. He also had uncompleted goals and was discouraged. Ruth had selected tapes for him to listen to on the beach, and they talked about the thousands of young people arising to do the Lord's work. This greatly encouraged the two of them, she said. As they rested, her husband's spirits rebounded.

Many people return home from vacation more exhausted than when they left. But Ruth reminded us that the word *rest* in Scripture means "refresh," not merely "relax." She compared Psalm 55:6 ("Oh, that I had wings like a dove! I would fly away and be at rest") with Isaiah 40:31 ("Those who wait on the LORD shall renew their strength; they shall mount up with wings like eagles" [NKJV]). Some people race off like doves to escape the pressure and fly back exhausted. But when we take breaks for resting and waiting on the Lord, we soar home like eagles, renewed.

Ruth asked if we'd noticed from Scripture that Philemon was

a "refreshing" Christian. Paul wrote, "Your love has given me great joy and encouragement, because you, brother, have refreshed the hearts of the Lord's people." He went on to plead, "Refresh my heart in Christ" (vv. 7, 20).

You can only refresh others if you're refreshed yourself, Ruth said. She recommended we study the word *refresh* in our Bibles.

When we asked Ruth about Bible study, she said that for her it was like being wide-eyed travelers in the midst of wonders. What makes scriptures meaningful is when we apply them to our own lives. There are many fruitful methods of Bible study, she said. Her advice was to try them all and, in reading other works, to vary our diet. We should use the Bible for home base, she said, but read, read, read anything else of value that we could.

She also advised us to read old books. She quoted C. S. Lewis: "It is a good rule, after reading a new book, never to allow yourself another new one till you have read an old one in between."[2] Ruth said that while she did read newer books, she always went back to those from prior generations, particularly Puritan writings, and the works of authors such as F. W. Boreham, whose books she collected. She also recommended missionary biographies.

She went on to tell us that Bible study is enhanced by pen and paper. We get more from our study when we take notes and record our observations. Cultivate the notebook habit, she said.

She showed us her notebook, saying she had a leather crafter who rebound it as necessary. Here, she said, she recorded her journal entries, stories she had heard, quotes she had found, and the lessons God was teaching her. As we record insights from our Bible studies, she noted, we are compiling our own personal Bible commentary.

Later that weekend Ruth spoke of the power of prayer as a daily habit. God loves to be reminded of His promises, she said. He never rebukes us for asking too much. She quoted a stanza from hymnist John Newton:

> *Thou art coming to a King,*
> *Large petitions with thee bring,*
> *For His grace and power are such,*
> *None can ever ask too much.*[3]

We asked what to do when we don't feel like praying. Pray when you feel like it, she replied, because it's wrong to neglect such an opportunity. Pray when you don't feel like it because it's dangerous to remain in such a condition.

The next day I told her I wanted to be a preacher and asked if she had any advice. Preach expository sermons, she said, keep them short, and use a lot of illustrations. Expository sermons, she explained, tackle the Bible paragraph by paragraph in logical sequence, allowing each verse to be studied in context. When we teach the Bible systematically, it reduces the chance of merely preaching our own opinions.

In preaching, she said, use much Scripture. And don't neglect preparation time. Though it wasn't always possible, she admitted, her husband sometimes spent weeks on one message.

She then described the 1949 Los Angeles crusade that launched Dr. Graham's worldwide ministry. When organizers kept extending the meetings, he ran out of sermons. He borrowed some from local pastors, and when he had used those up, he just read Scripture and said a few words. They weren't great sermons at all, she said, but still the people came.

I asked her about my anxiety and frequent low spirits. She reminded me of the story of the twelve spies Moses sent to reconnoiter the promised land. Ten brought back a bad report: the challenges were too hard, the giants too large, and the enemy too strong. But two—Joshua and Caleb—encouraged the people to possess the land. The difference between the ten spies and the two? The ten compared themselves with the giants, she said, but the two compared the giants with God.

Billy and Ruth Graham are in heaven now, but I will always remember what a refreshing couple they were. They had a remarkable way of helping people draw nearer to God. We can do the same. Find those who are closer to God than you are, and study their lives. Ask their secrets. Read their biographies. Learn from them, and then pass along the lessons to others.

As we draw closer to God, we'll pull people after us, as though a magnetic force were passing through us. Like Katrina, we'll brighten up the intensive care units of life. Like Mrs. Graham, we'll overflow with delightful lessons for others. Like Philemon, we'll refresh the hearts of the Lord's people.

Billy and Ruth Graham are in heaven now, but I will always remember what a refreshing couple they were.

By the way, I took Ruth's advice and looked up what the Bible said about refreshing people. When I did, I found a great biblical reference to the nearness of God: "Repent therefore, and turn back, that your sins may be blotted out, that times of refreshing may come from the presence of the Lord" (Acts 3:19–20 ESV).

I also found these verses, just for you:

"I will refresh the weary and satisfy the faint."

JEREMIAH 31:25

The law of the LORD is perfect, refreshing the soul.

PSALM 19:7

You gave abundant showers, O God;
   you refreshed your weary inheritance.

PSALM 68:9

He refreshes my soul. He guides me along the right paths.

PSALM 23:3

A generous person will prosper; whoever refreshes others will be refreshed.

PROVERBS 11:25

Refresh those who become exhausted in the wilderness.

2 SAMUEL 16:2

They refreshed my spirit and yours also. Such men deserve recognition.

1 CORINTHIANS 16:18

part seven

delight

in Special Places

God's Exceedingly Entertaining Creation

God created the universe to convey His majesty. That's why we feel close to God in nature: hiking in the mountains, sailing on the lake, walking on the beach. When we find Christ, we find the Creator, and He sets our hearts on fire. Jonathan Edwards said, following his conversion:

> As I was walking there, and looked up on the sky and clouds, there came into my mind, so sweet a sense of the glorious majesty and grace of God, that I know not how to express [it]. . . .

The appearance of everything was altered, there seemed to be, as it were, a calm, sweet cast, or appearance of divine glory, in almost every thing. God's excellency, his wisdom, his purity and love, seemed to appear in every thing; in the sun, moon, and stars; in the clouds, and blue sky; in the grass, flowers, trees; in the water, and all nature.[1]

Edwards, who had been terrified of storms, now rejoiced in them. "I felt God at the first appearance of a thunder-storm," he said, and he took "the opportunity . . . to view the clouds, and see the lightnings play, and hear the majestic and awful voice of God's thunder, which often times was exceeding entertaining, leading me to sweet contemplations of my great and glorious God."[2]

All the universe is God's habitation, and His creation is exceedingly entertaining to His children. We delight in watching water plunge over the falls, penguins waddle over the ice, and snow carpet the mountains.

Yet some places are special. The most emotional times in life are usually associated with specific places—the home where we grew up; the church where we were baptized; the overlook where we proposed; the little cove where we turned over a problem to the Lord; the chapel where we were married; the cemetery where a dear one is buried.

Jesus had such a place, a walled garden on the eastern slopes of Jerusalem. Apparently a friend owned an olive grove called Gethsemane, and John 18 tells us Jesus often went there. On the last night of His natural life, Jesus prayed among its ancient trees in the moonlight.

Throughout the Bible, people had their special places of worship. They built altars. They erected monuments. They constructed temples. For Moses, an ordinary tent in the wilderness became an extraordinary place of fellowship with God.

> Moses used to take a tent and pitch it outside the camp some distance way, calling it the "tent of meeting." Anyone inquiring of the LORD would go to the tent of meeting outside the camp. . . . As Moses went into the tent, the pillar of cloud would come down and stay at the entrance, while the LORD spoke with Moses. . . . The LORD would speak to Moses face to face, as one speaks to a friend. . . . When Aaron and all the Israelites saw Moses, his face was radiant. (Exodus 33:7, 9, 11; 34:30)

That's the common experience of uncommon Jesus-followers. We find places where we can draw near to God and talk with Him face-to-face, as a person speaks with a friend. When we draw aside to meet with the Lord, He descends and meets with us, and our faces glow from His radiance. That can happen anywhere, anytime.

At a memorial service for evangelist D. L. Moody, an associate said, "He walked with God, and so did not have to turn out of his way to speak to Him. I have been driving with him off on some retired road about Northfield. We would be talking together, when, suddenly, he would pause for a moment and speak to God just as naturally as he would speak to his friend."[3]

God is near wherever we are, but some places are special. We need to stake out some holy ground where our divine connection affects our human complexions. When we have been with our Father, it should show on our faces. The Bible says:

> We all, with unveiled face, beholding as in a mirror the glory
> of the Lord, are being transformed into the same image from

When we draw aside to meet with the Lord, He descends and meets with us, and our faces glow from His radiance.

glory to glory, just as by the Spirit of the Lord. (2 Corinthians 3:18 NKJV)

Those who look to him are radiant. (Psalm 34:5)

The Nearness
of My God

Psalm 73:28 says, "But as for me, it is good to be near God." This was written by Asaph, a man upset at his government and its corrupt leaders. He began Psalm 73 saying, "Surely God is good to Israel, to those who are pure in heart. But as for me, my feet had almost slipped. . . . I envied the arrogant" (vv. 1–3).

Asaph's foes were raking in money and boasting about it. Meanwhile, he said, "They have no struggles; their bodies are healthy and strong. They are free from common human burdens" (vv. 4–5). These power brokers were defrauding the poor and abusing the weak. "From their callous hearts comes iniquity," said Asaph. "Their evil imaginations have no limit" (v. 7). When Asaph spoke to them of spiritual things, they scoffed, saying, "How would God know? Does the Most High know anything?" (v. 11).

Asaph, one of their victims, couldn't understand why God allowed such inequity. "When I tried to understand all this," he said in verse 16, "it troubled me deeply till I entered the sanctuary of God," he said. "Then I understood their final destiny" (v. 17).

Asaph had a spiritual breakthrough when he finally went into the temple courts and processed the situation in the presence of God. When he reviewed the truth of God's Word, he realized that evildoers are here today and gone tomorrow. "How suddenly are they destroyed, completely swept away by terrors! They are like a dream when one awakes" (vv. 19–20).

Based on God's perspective, Asaph calmed himself. He ended the psalm remembering the privilege of being close to God and living in His presence—something the wicked never experience.

> Yet I am always with you;
>> you hold me by my right hand.
> You guide me with your counsel,
>> and afterward you will take me into glory.
> Whom have I in heaven but you?
>> And earth has nothing I desire besides you.
> My flesh and my heart may fail,

but God is the strength of my heart
and my portion forever.
Those who are far from you will perish;
you destroy all who are unfaithful to you.
But as for me, it is good to be near God.
I have made the Sovereign LORD my refuge;
I will tell of all your deeds. (Psalm 73:23–28)

Whenever you're overwhelmed with confusion, make a trip to the temple—it might be a kitchen table or a mountain pathway—and process matters in the light of biblical truth. This is the only sure way to move from embittered pain to empowered praise.

Ask Not for Whom the Bell Tolls

There are a handful of sacred places in my life. One is Harris Memorial Church in Greene County, Tennessee. Last summer Katrina and I retraced the rural roads of East Tennessee to the place where we began pastoral ministry on our first wedding anniversary. My salary was $97.50 a week, plus potatoes, tomatoes, and love.

The little church is constructed of river rock with a rich wooden interior. A cemetery rings one side, and on the other side is a belfry containing a heavy cast iron bell. Every Sunday as the morning service began, I stepped onto the exterior stoop. Grasping the bell cord, which ran through a pipe behind the stonework, I would pull the rope and send the bell swinging side to side. Soon its venerable tones would echo through the mountains, calling the valley to worship.

One blistering Sunday, dressed in my suit and with sermon in hand, I stepped onto the stoop and grasped the rope. I gave a gentle pull, but it didn't move. It seemed caught on something. I gave a harder tug. Nothing happened. Finally, gripping the rope more tightly, I yanked the cord with all my might. I heard a scraping sound, and suddenly the heavy bell tumbled out of the belfry, plummeted past my nose, and broke the concrete steps at my feet.

> Suddenly the heavy bell tumbled out of the belfry, plummeted past my nose, and broke the concrete steps at my feet.

Everyone inside the church ran to the windows to see the commotion. There I stood, Bible in one hand and limp rope in the other. At my feet, the bell lay more broken than the one in Philadelphia. Had I been standing a half step closer, it would have cracked my skull.

That's not the only time I nearly lost my life in that brief pastorate. One night, when Katrina got up to check on our baby, she found the house on fire. We scooped up the baby and escaped as the house burned down around us.

Through thick and thin, the good people of Harris Memorial Church stood with us. Katrina and I stayed there for more than two years, until a larger church hired us. We packed our belongings with mixed emotions, and at last the day came for us to leave. My old deacon, I. L. Stanley, who had become a mentor, came to see us off. We had grown close. Every week I had driven to his cabin in the woods to review my next sermon with him. He always prayed with me and loved me.

As we were about to slip away, Mr. Stanley drove into the yard. Lumbering from his truck, he gripped my arm, his eyes wet, and finally said, "I thought you might have stayed with us a little longer."

He spoke out of love, but his words broke my heart. I can still hear them echoing in my memory and have seldom spoken of them. It's one of the reasons I've stayed at my second church for forty years. Somehow God spoke to me about stability, permanence, and ties that bind our hearts in Christian love.

As we go through life, there are certain places where we meet God, make friends, learn lessons, find strength, reach decisions, change direction, solidify commitment, and hear the voice of the Lord.

In the Old Testament, Samuel built a monument to commemorate a God-given victory for Israel. Samuel called it Ebenezer—"Thus far the LORD has helped us," or as the King James Version says, "Hitherto hath the LORD helped us" (1 Samuel 7:12).

It's important to build Ebenezers in our lives to remind ourselves that our Friend Unseen, who has led us this far, won't leave us now. It's wonderful to look back over life, despite our failures, to see a series of mile markers, all testifying to one fact: Jesus has led us all the way. Thank God for moments that have become monuments to His goodness, and for places He transforms into holy ground.

> *Here I raise my Ebenezer*
> *Hither by Thy help I've come,*
> *And I hope by Thy good pleasure*
> *Safely to arrive at home.*
>
> ROBERT ROBINSON, "COME, THOU
> FOUNT OF EVERY BLESSING"

part eight

delight

in Challenging Moments

Into the Sand

F. W. Boreham used to tell of a framed scrap of paper on his parents' wall saying, "Hitherto Hath the Lord Helped Us." One day he asked his mother about it, and she told of a time she and her husband had faced a crisis. She'd been distressed for weeks, but one day, pacing back and forth, she paused in front of the calendar on the wall. "The only thing I saw was the text in the corner," she said. "It was as if someone had spoken the words. 'Hitherto has the Lord helped us.' I was so overcome I sat down and had a good cry; and then I began again with a fresh heart and trust."[1]

The God who has been your help in ages past is your hope for years to come. The Lord will stay near you, especially in critical times. Psalm 34:18 says, "The LORD is close to the brokenhearted and saves those who are crushed in spirit."

He draws near us, both in life's major agitations and in our daily aggravations.

I'm writing this chapter in Ghana, where today I met a man from Ethiopia who told me his story. When he was thirteen and in the eighth grade, he was singing in Sunday school. Suddenly, soldiers burst into the building and arrested the children. He was imprisoned three weeks and nine days. Prison authorities demanded that he renounce his faith in Christ, and he was forced to roll in the sand, which was coarse like glass and painful. If he stopped rolling, he was whipped.

"What did your imprisonment do for you?" I asked.

"It brought me closer to God," he said. "When I went into prison, I had my parents' faith, but when I came out of prison it was *my* faith." Today this man is a pastor in Ethiopia, and his face glowed as he told the story.[2] Though my friend's story is unique, the lesson he learned is common to all God's children. We often draw closer to Him during times of difficulty, and the trials of life make His presence real to us in a way that strengthens our faith.

> The God who has been your help in ages past is your hope for years to come.

- When Joseph was imprisoned in Egypt, the Bible says, "the LORD was with him" (Genesis 39:3, 21).
- When the three Hebrew children were thrown into Nebuchadnezzar's fiery furnace in Daniel 3, the Lord descended on a beam of light and walked among the flames as the fourth man (v. 25).
- When the twelve disciples battled the elements, Jesus drew near, walking on the water and shouting over the storm, "Take courage! It is I. Don't be afraid" (Matthew 14:27).
- When Paul was imprisoned in Jerusalem, "the Lord stood near Paul and said, 'Take courage!'" (Acts 23:11).
- When Jesus faced the loneliest night of His life, He said, "Yet I am not alone, for my Father is with me" (John 16:32).

The Lord knows how to join us in the valleys and furnaces, when we feel imprisoned by grief or tormented by loneliness. The Lord is close to the brokenhearted. He said, "When you pass through the waters, I will be with you; and when you pass through the rivers, they will not sweep over you. When you walk through the fire, you will not be burned; the flames will not set you ablaze. For I am the LORD your God . . . your Savior" (Isaiah 43:2–3).

Sometimes our difficulties aren't catastrophic; they're just, well, claustrophobic. We're not always rolling in coarse sand. Sometimes we're stuck in the basement.

For our thirty-fifth anniversary, Katrina and I decided to go to Paris. We weren't sure we could make a trip like that, given her disability. But I had frequent-flyer miles, and we found a handicap-accessible hotel. The easiest way from the airport to our hotel was the Métro, we were told, so upon arriving at Charles de Gaulle Airport, we found and boarded the train into town. The trip had exhausted us, but we were nearly to our destination. When we reached the downtown station, we arrived on a basement level, and the elevator had an Out of Service sign.

"What's wrong with the elevator?" I asked an attendant.

"It's not working today, monsieur," she said.

"Can someone help with it?"

"It is not possible. You should have called ahead."

"Called ahead? How did I know the elevator wasn't working?" She shrugged.

"We're stranded below street level," I said, "and my wife's in a wheelchair. What do you suggest we do?"

"You will have to go back to the airport and take a taxi."

"Go back to the airport!"

The woman simply walked away. I looked at another attendant

and said, "I'm going to carry my wife up those stairs, and I could use some help."

"It is not permitted for you to do that," he said.

"Yes, but I'm going to do it anyway and would appreciate your help."

I gripped Katrina's wheelchair and started for the staircase. When I stooped to lift her into my arms, there he was. I asked him to grab the wheelchair, and a couple of passersby took our backpacks. I scooped Katrina into my arms, and she gripped my neck. It took all our strength, but we ascended those steps one at a time, from the basement to the landing, and from the landing to the street. The agent scampered up the steps ahead of us, unfolded the wheelchair, and helped Katrina get seated. The passersby returned our backpacks. We thanked them, tipped the attendant, found our hotel, and had no more difficulty the entire trip.

We took a lot of pictures that week and made a lot of memories. If only we had a picture of that uphill climb! That's the moment

That's when we felt closest, her in my arms, hers around my neck, gripping each other and defying the gravity of the moment.

we most remember about the trip. That's when we felt closest, her in my arms, hers around my neck, gripping each other and defying the gravity of the moment.

I believe the Lord was carrying us both. He does that, you know. Deuteronomy 1:30–31 says, "The LORD your God, who is going before you, will fight for you, as he did for you in Egypt, before your very eyes, and in the wilderness. There you saw how the LORD your God carried you, as a father carries his son, all the way you went until you reached this place."

The uphill climbs of life are often the moments we cherish later. It's when we're rolling in the sand that our faith becomes our own. It's when we're stuck in the basement that the Lord carries us to a higher level—if we'll simply grip Him tightly and hang on.

> You hem me in behind and before,
>   and you lay your hand upon me.
> Such knowledge is too wonderful for me. . . .
> Even the darkness will not be dark to you.
>
> PSALM 139:5–6, 12

Into the Light

My first experience with grief was when Tippy died, the little dog that rode in my bicycle basket. I had never felt such hurt and didn't know it existed. My dad took me in his lap, held me, let me cry, and talked to me. He told me Tippy had gotten old, had lost most of his teeth, could hardly eat, and that it was time for him to go to dog heaven. How long he held me, I don't know; but that may have been his most fatherly moment with me, and his closeness wrapped me with comfort.

Not everyone has such a father, but we all have access to a heavenly Father who specializes in comforting us in sorrow and embracing us with promises. The Bible says:

- "I, even I, am he who comforts you." (Isaiah 51:12)
- "Praise be to the God and Father of our Lord Jesus Christ, the Father of compassion and the God of all comfort, who comforts us all in our troubles." (2 Corinthians 1:3–4)
- "I remember, LORD, your ancient laws, and I find comfort in them. . . . May your unfailing love be my comfort." (Psalm 119:52, 76)

The time-tested way to crawl into the Father's lap and receive His comfort involves giving Him the problems we cannot solve, the burdens we cannot bear, and the work we cannot do. Psalm 55:22 says, "Cast your cares on the LORD and he will sustain you; he will never let the righteous be shaken." Peter wrote, "Cast all your anxiety on him because he cares for you" (1 Peter 5:7).

Matilda Jane Evans described this process so completely there's no doubt she wrote from experience. Matilda immigrated to South Australia in 1852 and married a local minister. Their life was hard, and Matilda began writing books to keep food on the table. She authored novels under the pen name Maud Jeanne Franc and became the Australian Jane Austen. Her book *Into the Light* tells the story of Bessie Bruce, who was tormented with fear for her brother, Sid. After being jilted by the woman he loved, Sid's health had broken and he appeared to be dying. He had no spiritual hope. Bessie wrote:

My worst fears were magnified in my own mind. I ran to my little room, and, closing and locking the door, threw myself on the floor by the side of the large chair, and burying my head in the cushions, gave way to an agony of weeping. The burden of my cry for a long time was only the words, "My brother! Oh, my brother!" I remembered nothing but my fears—my brother slowly going from me, I to be left behind. The cloud had gathered in blackness overhead.

Then came a little uplifting of the cloud. "What had God promised?" I lay there thinking it over. Why, He had promised help in the time of trouble, and I was forgetting to call upon Him. He had bid me cast my burden upon Him, and

> The time-tested way to crawl into the Father's lap and receive His comfort involves giving Him the problems we cannot solve, the burdens we cannot bear, and the work we cannot do.

had promised to sustain; and here was I bearing my own burden. Bearing it? No, but crushed down—prostrated beneath it.

Was this honoring God? Was this taking my Father at His word?

I rose and went to the window, and kneeling upon the broad seat, with my elbows on the sill, looked down on the broad expanse of vines stretching before me, fresh and beautiful, with abundant promise of fruit—and the spreading peach-trees; and the memory of God's goodness came over me like an overwhelming flood.

Then, like a little child, I bowed before Him and told Him all my trouble, reminding Him of His word—how He had promised that none should ask anything touching His kingdom, and go unanswered. I asked with all my heart for a blessing on my brother; his health was not all. That, I felt, with God's will, might easily come with his soul's health. My cry was for light—that his darkness be dispelled and that the shining Sun of Righteousness might rise on him.

I arose reassured and refreshed, wondering, too, that after so many proofs of God's goodness I had so soon forgotten my Best Friend in my heaviest need. And in the silence of my room that night I blessed God and took courage.[1]

What a picture of casting our cares on Him who cares for us! When we learn to do that, we can bless God and take courage. The psalmist said, "From the end of the earth I will cry to You, when my heart is overwhelmed; lead me to the rock that is higher than I" (Psalm 61:2 NKJV).

Nothing is easier to do—and nothing is harder. I've had to repeatedly come to the Lord with burdens that were crushing me. But I have never known a time when He did not draw me near, fatherlike, in moments of fear and sorrow.

Don't cast a few of your burdens on the Lord. Don't even cast most of them on Him. The Bible says, "Cast *all* your anxiety on him because he cares for you" (1 Peter 5:7, emphasis added).

That means the one you're most worried about right now.

delight

in Unseen Realities

Don't Lose Heart

On August 12, 1865, Jimmy Greenlees, eleven, was hit by a carriage in Glasgow, snapping his leg in several places. Almost immediately, infection set in. Most doctors would have amputated Jimmy's leg, inviting more infection and likely death. But the house surgeon that day was Dr. Joseph Lister, who believed in the invisible world of germs. Other doctors laughed at him, but Dr. Lister was not one to lose heart. He'd concocted a method of using carbolic acid to kill the hypothetical germs but had never tried it on a human. He did that day. Lister bathed Jimmy's leg in a solution of carbolic acid and for several days kept the bandage wet with the solution. When he removed the bandage, he was overjoyed. No pus, no odor, no infection. The boy recovered fully, and a new page was added to medical history.

Even so, many doctors refused to believe in germs because they could not see them. Fifteen years later, when President James Garfield was shot in Washington, the doctors treating him rejected Lister's theories. Garfield died, not so much from the assassin's bullets as from the malpractice of his medical team.[1]

But Dr. Joseph Lister, a follower of Christ, knew the power of invisible realities.

In some ways, that defines Christ-followers. We are people who know of an unseen world, which we glimpse through the lens of Scripture. This is what saves us from losing heart and giving up. Germs were never invisible, of course; they were simply beyond the power of the naked eye. Nor are the unseen realities of God truly invisible. They are beyond our present vision, but wonderfully described in the Bible.

Second Corinthians 4:16–18 says, "Therefore we do not lose heart. Though outwardly we are wasting away, yet inwardly we are being renewed day by day. For our light and momentary troubles are achieving for us an eternal glory that far outweighs them all. So we fix our eyes not on what is seen, but on what is unseen, since what is seen is temporary, but what is unseen is eternal."

The book of 2 Corinthians is Paul's most autobiographical letter, in which he openly described his sufferings and fears. He began chapter 4 saying, "Therefore, since through God's mercy we have this ministry, we do not lose heart. . . . We are hard pressed on every side, but not crushed; perplexed, but not in despair; persecuted, but not abandoned; struck down, but not destroyed" (vv. 1, 8–9).

Paul repeated himself, for emphasis, in verse 16: "Therefore we do not lose heart."

I don't know what burden you're bearing, what trial you're facing, or what problem you're up against. But I know God doesn't want you to lose heart. Many times I could have given up, but the Lord never let me—that's the testimony of everyone who lives by unseen realities.

God keeps His people spiritually vibrant through His invisible realities, and our problems, even the worst of them, are—these are God's words—"light and momentary" (v. 17). I don't want to minimize what you're going through. I've had problems that have demolished me; they seemed anything but light and momentary. But God's perspective is different from ours. He knows the end from the beginning, and from His vantage point our problems are but a bump in the road.

All your problems are temporary, but all God's promises are eternal. His truth will outlive your trials. Romans 8:18 says, "I consider that our present sufferings are not worth comparing with the glory that will be revealed in us."

Suppose someone gave you an estate in Malibu with beautiful views of the Pacific. The home had an infinity swimming pool, breathtaking terraces, and fabulous landscaping. Imagine you flew to California, where a limousine met you. But on the freeway the car hit a pothole and drove through a rough patch of pavement that shook you up a little. That would have been unsettling, but it couldn't compare to the exhilaration of driving through the gates of your new home.

All your problems are temporary, but all God's promises are eternal.

As we journey toward our heavenly home, we hit potholes and rough patches. We have delays, worries, even crises and tragedies. Yet we can say on the authority of Scripture that they are not worth comparing to the glory to be revealed. Our light and momentary troubles are achieving for us an eternal glory that far outweighs them all.

That's why we don't lose heart. The whole world is focused on the visible, but those who follow Christ concentrate on the unseen. We delight in God's nearness, and we revel in the company of our Friend Unseen.

Build your hopes on things eternal,
Hold to God's unchanging hand.

JENNIE B. WILSON, "HOLD TO GOD'S UNCHANGING HAND"

The Unseen Friend

Nineteenth-century poet Lucy Larcom wrote in *The Unseen Friend*, "There is no life so poor as that which has lost all conscious hold upon unseen realities. . . . When we are aware of an Eternal Life encircling us, of which we are a part, of a Loving Presence within us to whom we belong, simply to be alive is almost an overpowering blessedness."

"Our life is fed," she said, "from unseen sources."[1]

Hebrews 11:27 says of Moses, "By faith he left Egypt, not fearing the king's anger; he persevered because he saw him who is invisible." Jesus-followers live by unseen realities, and our personalities are fed from invisible resources. We persevere, seeing Him who is invisible. Yes, we are realists; we know what's going on. But we center our attention on the unseen and the eternal:

- *Our invisible Father.* According to John 1:18, no one has ever seen God. Yet Jesus told us, "Pray to your Father, who is unseen" (Matthew 6:6). He hears us, and He is worthy of our praise. Paul wrote, "Now unto the King eternal, immortal, invisible, the only wise God, be honour and glory for ever and ever" (1 Timothy 1:17 KJV).
- *His unseen Son.* Jesus told His disciples, "I am going to the Father, where you can see me no longer" (John 16:10). Peter later wrote, "Though you have not seen him, you love him" (1 Peter 1:8). He is currently out of our range of vision, but one day we will see our Lord face-to-face.
- *The Holy Spirit.* Jesus likened the Holy Spirit to the wind, saying, "The wind blows wherever it pleases. You hear its sound, but you cannot tell where it comes from or where it is going" (John 3:8). Invisible though He is, we know it is He who "helps us in our weakness" and "intercedes for us" (Romans 8:26).
- *God's attributes.* Romans 1:20 speaks of "God's invisible qualities—his eternal power and divine nature." All His traits are invisible to us—His justice, mercy, power, love, holiness, changelessness, authority, truthfulness, faithfulness. Yet these attributes hold the universe together, and us too.

- *Our heavenly home.* We cannot see heaven; it is concealed from our vision for now, but it is a real place. Jesus promised, "I am going there to prepare a place for you" (John 14:2), and the Bible provides wonderful descriptions of it to fuel our anticipation, as one day it will be our eternal home.

- *The angels of God.* Thirty-nine books of the Bible contain references to angels, and their activity spans Scripture from Genesis to Revelation. The Bible speaks of good angels and fallen ones, including the devil himself. A spiritual grid surrounds our planet, and an angelic hierarchy inhabits the universe. It's as real as any government on earth.[2] For those who love Christ, God's angels are "ministering spirits sent to serve those who will inherit salvation" (Hebrews 1:14).

- *The fulfillment of God's precious promises.* Hebrews 11:1 says, "Now faith is confidence in what we hope for and assurance about what we do not see." The Lord has given us promises to cover every contingency in life. These are the most beloved scriptures to our souls. They are the basis of our life of faith, these "exceedingly great and precious promises" (2 Peter 1:4 NKJV). But they unfold over time. They direct our attention to a future moment when God will do exactly as He has said in His Word.

We are deluged by the visible—a world in chaos, a nation divided, financial struggles, family problems, physical ailments. We never know what a day will bring. When our focus is limited to the visible, we grow frightened. But when we realize invisible realities are at play, we cannot lose heart. With spiritual eyes we see the Father, the Son, and the Holy Spirit. We see God's holy angels surrounding the earth. We trust in the qualities of God. We believe God's promises and wait with earnest expectation for their unstoppable fulfillment. And we yearn for heaven. These unseen realities are greater than the negative realities surrounding us day by day.

Charles Spurgeon said, "You are looking too much to the things that are seen, and too little to your unseen Friend. In an unseen Savior we fix our trust, from an unseen Savior we derive our joy. Our faith is now the substance of things hoped for, the evidence of things not seen."[3]

When you awaken each morning, envision God standing there to greet you. As you drive to work, speak to Him naturally, as if

> With spiritual eyes we see the Father, the Son, and the Holy Spirit. We see God's holy angels surrounding the earth.

He were in the passenger seat. Before an appointment, whisper a prayer for His help. As you relax at the end of the day, your work behind you, remember the angels hovering near. As you turn down the covers of your bed, remember you are blanketed with the promises of God. As you fall asleep, ponder your heavenly home.

God is so much closer than you know, and His unseen grace will, in His timing, overturn all of life's unseemly moments.

part ten

delight

*in Doing the
Next Thing*

Cheered by the
Presence of God

Recently I made the hardest decision in my professional life—to leave the role that had been my life's work. I loved everything I was doing, but I couldn't continue doing it all. I felt debilitated. Preparing sermons each week. Directing a staff. Resolving conflicts. Caring for so many. Raising money and overseeing the machinery of a growing organization.

All that, I could have done. But I was also maintaining a strenuous writing and speaking schedule. And my family was increasing—grandchildren everywhere.

Still, I think I could have managed it with God's help.

But in 2010, Katrina had surgery to replace a heart valve, and things changed. Until then, she could transfer herself from bed to chair, and from chair to shower. But after surgery she was unable to recover her baseline mobility, and I became more involved in caregiving. This included, as I learned, grocery shopping, bed making, dish washing, bathroom scrubbing, oven cleaning, recipe gathering, bill paying, and tossing items out of the refrigerator with expiration dates older than me.

The fatigue made me irritable, and my impatience made Katrina feel, understandably, hurt. We were both battling multiple sclerosis, and I realize now we were both coping with loss. While our love and marriage never faltered, we had to learn to become caregivers, each to the other.

I began praying in detail about my work. I prayed for five years, sketching a hand-drawn calendar into my notebook, looking ahead, noting milestones, thinking, anticipating how the future might look. When the Lord gave me peace about His timing, I met with my board and told them that while I didn't want to leave my church—unless they desired—I felt I should shift roles. The church created a new job for me, and this gave Katrina and me breathing space without removing us from those we loved. God walked with us through the process, and I learned once again that we're never closer to Him than when we take each step in stride with Him.

In my book *The Red Sea Rules*, I described how the Israelites were trapped at the Red Sea in Exodus 14, yet God told them to take the next logical step by faith. They were to go forward. As they did, the waters parted, and God made a way for them. "Just think of it," I wrote. "The winds blew, the sea split, the waters congealed into towering walls, and the Israelites pass through dry-shod."[1]

I learned once again that we're never closer to Him than when we take each step in stride with Him.

The same God who led them in led them out.

Taking the next step by faith thwarts our tendency to worry ourselves sick. You can't easily solve large problems; they will pulverize you. But there is usually some little step you can take, and that's all that's required for now. You can't instantly complete overwhelming tasks, but you can tackle the next thing to be done. God keeps stride with our short steps.

When the Israelites were trying to rebuild the destroyed temple in Jerusalem, the work seemed pitiful. The Lord told the workers, "Who of you is left who saw this house in its former glory? How does it look to you now? Does it not seem to you like nothing? But now be strong. . . . Be strong. . . . Be strong . . . and work. For I am with you" (Haggai 2:3–4).

"People who have themselves experienced both grief and fear know how alike those two things are," wrote Elisabeth Elliot. "They know the restlessness and loss of appetite, the inability to concentrate, the inner silent wail that cannot be muffled. . . . At such a time, I have been wonderfully calmed and strengthened by doing some simple duty. Nothing valiant or meritorious or spiritual at all—just something that needed to be done, like a bed to be freshly made or a kitchen floor to be scrubbed. . . . Sometimes it takes everything you have to tackle the job, but it is surprising how strength comes."[2]

She continued, "There is wonderful therapy in taking oneself by the scruff of the neck, getting up, and doing something. While you are doing, time passes quickly. Time itself will in some measure heal, and 'light arises in the darkness'—slowly, it seems but certainly."[3]

The Lord is anything but lazy. He is never in a hurry, but His purposes ripen and His promises unfold in His timing. We seldom know what He wants us to do a year from now, or ten or twenty. We can't even be sure of tomorrow. But we can usually figure out what to do today, and the next thing is all we can do. The Bible offers this counsel:

- "Commit to the LORD whatever you do, and he will establish your plans." (Proverbs 16:3)
- "Whatever you do, whether in word or deed, do it all in the

name of the Lord Jesus, giving thanks to God the Father
through him." (Colossians 3:17)
- "Whatever you do, work at it with all your heart, as
  working for the Lord." (Colossians 3:23)
- "So whether you eat or drink or whatever you do, do it all
  for the glory of God." (1 Corinthians 10:31)

These "whatever you do" verses are some of the most practical
in the Bible. Heed them! Don't just lie there and let the devil attack
you. Don't sit around feeling anxious. Don't sink in depression. Get
up and do the next thing. And whatever you do, commit it to the
Lord. Do it in the name of Jesus, with all your heart, as unto Him
and for His glory.

George MacDonald said, "The performance of small duties,
yes, even of the smallest, will do more to give temporary repose,
will act more as healthful [medicines], than the greatest joys that
can come to us from any other quarter."[4]

The French monk François de La Mothe wrote a paragraph
that has become a working philosophy for my life, and I recom-
mend it to you:

Cheered by the presence of God, I will do at each moment,
without anxiety, according to the strength which He shall give

me, the work that His Providence assigns me. I will leave the rest without concern; it is not my affair. I ought to consider the duty to which I am called each day, as the work that God has given me to do, and to apply myself to it in a manner worthy of His glory, that is to say, in exactness and peace.[5]

With the Lord Forever

Jesus died and rose again so He could be near us forever. He told the thief on the cross, "Today you will be with Me in Paradise" (Luke 23:43 NKJV). That one sentence made the thief's last day on earth his first day in heaven, and the worst moment he'd ever known became the greatest joy he'd ever experienced. In an instant he went from tortured gasps to shouts of glory.

The apostle Paul described death as being "home with the Lord" (2 Corinthians 5:8). He said, "We will be with the Lord forever" (1 Thessalonians 4:17); and, "Now we see only a reflection as in a mirror; then we shall see face to face" (1 Corinthians 13:12).

I'm homesick to see my parents again and those whom I love

who've gone before me, but shouldn't I want to see our Savior most of all? Shouldn't you?

My favorite biblical passage about heaven is Revelation 21–22, the concluding chapters of Scripture, which provide the Bible's most complete picture of our eternal home. The emphasis running through these chapters is the perpetual access we'll have to our Creator.

Look at how Revelation 21 begins: "I saw the Holy City, the new Jerusalem, coming down out of heaven from God. . . . And I heard a loud voice from the throne saying, 'Look! God's dwelling place is now *among the people*, and *he will dwell with them. They will be his people*, and *God himself will be with them* and be their God'" (vv. 2–3, emphasis added).

The rest of Revelation 21 describes the city of New Jerusalem: its size, its walls, its colors, its light, and its dazzling purity. Revelation 22:1–4 takes us to the very center of the city, saying, "Then the angel showed me the river of the water of life, as clear as crystal, flowing from the throne of God and of the Lamb down the middle of the great street of the city. . . . The throne of God and of the Lamb will be in the city, and his servants will serve him. They will see his face."

If anything is greater than the *grace* of Jesus, it's the *face* of Jesus, and Revelation 22:4 leaves no question that we will see His face.

First John 3:2 makes the same point: "We know that when Christ appears, we shall be like him for we shall see him as he is."

Stephen, the first martyr of the church, got a preview. As he collapsed in death, the Bible says he "looked up to heaven and saw the glory of God, and Jesus standing at the right hand of God" (Acts 7:55).

I'm convinced the biblical descriptions of the heavenly city are authentic. They are as literal as the resurrected body of the Lord Jesus, who stepped from the tomb and ascended to heaven physically and materially. We will literally, physically, bodily, tangibly, visually see our Lord and be with Him forever, and throughout eternity we'll have lots of one-on-one fellowship with the One who died for us and rose again.

If anything is greater than the grace of Jesus, it's the face of Jesus.

Imagine! Face time with Jesus, forever, for you and me, in the new heavens, the new earth, and the city of New Jerusalem. At the end of human history, God will re-create the universe, and His great diamond city will descend in glory. At its center will be a throne, and on the throne will sit our God and Savior, reigning and ruling. As Fanny Crosby wrote, "I shall see Him face to face, and tell the story, saved by grace."

I wouldn't miss that for anything. Would you?

When we speak of the Lord's nearness, we mean two things: His presence is near, but so is His return. When the New Testament writers said, "The Lord is near," they sometimes spoke in terms of space, and sometimes in terms of time. He is near us presently, and His return is close at hand, for the times are reaching their fulfillment.

Whether today, tomorrow, or the day after, I don't know; but we've never been so close to the edge of history, and I'm anticipating the next step in the prophetic plan of God. The psalmist wrote, "You make known to me the path of life; you will fill me with joy in your presence, with eternal pleasures at your right hand" (Psalm 16:11).

With racing pulse, we await the next step—the summons home, the trumpet call—and the Bible gives us two prayers to offer along these lines:

"Maranatha—come, Lord!" (1 Corinthians 16:22, my translation)

"Amen. Come, Lord Jesus!" (Revelation 22:20)

Make it a habit to whisper these prayers whenever you see a gorgeous sunrise or a breathtaking sunset. Make it a point to study scriptural prophecy and the Bible's descriptions of eternity. Make it a rule to stoke your love for the Lord's return until you're ready, at His summons, to step off this planet and hasten your trip upward and onward, where we'll be ever near our Lord for billions and billions of years, and beyond. Hallelujah! And amen!

> *And Lord, haste the day when my faith shall be sight*
> *The clouds be rolled back as a scroll;*
> *The trump shall resound, and the Lord shall descend,*
> *Even so—it is well with my soul.*
>
> HORATIO SPAFFORD, "IT IS WELL WITH MY SOUL"

Acknowledgments

I don't recall my dad saying "Thank you" very often, but he was forever telling people, "Much obliged!" It was the Appalachian equivalent. So that's what I want to say:

To Katrina, who has shared the journey of this book. And to my daughters, sons-in-law, grandchildren, and to my sister and brother-in-law, all of whom are my closest friends and keep my emotional boiler stoked.

To those who let me share their experiences; and to mentors from whom I've learned much that's recorded here.

To my agents, Sealy and Matt Yates; to my assistant, Sherry Anderson; and to Joshua Rowe of Clearly Media, who, along with Kyle Saunders, has turned this book into printed and video curriculum for groups.

To Dr. David Jeremiah, who, over breakfast last year, told me something that caused me to put "a bit more of myself" into this book.

To the team at HarperCollins Gift Books. They are a small galaxy of remarkable people whose combined skills cause every word to sit on the page with authenticity and artistry, cover to cover. Thank you, Laura, LeeEric, Kristen, Michael, Mandy, and Stefanie.

And finally, to you, who persevered through this book to its final acknowledgments. Much obliged!

Notes

Introduction

1. June Wilkinson Hersey, in discussion with the author in 2018. Used with permission. This story is also affirmed by Dr. Kenneth Eagleton, missionary physician, who was present in the airport in São Paulo that evening.
2. "Just a Closer Walk with Thee" is a traditional American spiritual, authorship and date of composition unknown.

The Rabid Dog

1. E. Stanley Jones, *Abundant Living* (New York: Abingdon-Cokesbury Press, 1942), 76.
2. Dr. Harold P. Adolph, in discussion with the author in February 2017. Used with permission. Dr. Adolph also relates this story in

his book *What If There Were Windows in Heaven?* (Meadville, PA: Christian Faith Publishing, 2017), 15–16.

God's Two Addresses

1. Adapted from several sources, including the *San Francisco Call*, February 23, 1913, https://cdnc.ucr.edu/cgi-bin/cdnc?a=d&d =SFC19130223.2.131.4; and Ruth A. Tucker, *Stories of Faith* (Grand Rapids: Zondervan, 1989), 304.

2. Quoted by David Allen Park in *The Grand Contraption: The World as Myth, Number, and Chance* (Princeton, NJ: Princeton University Press, 2005), 159.

3. Quoted by Henry Adams, *Mont-Saint-Michel and Chartres* (Boston: Houghton Mifflin, 1913), 286.

4. Brother Lawrence, *The Practice of the Presence of God* (New York: Fleming H. Revell, 1895), 21; italics in original.

5. Brother Lawrence, 28.

Don't Be Afraid; I Am with You

1. Jim and Val Harvey, *What a Difference a Name Makes* (Bloomington, IN: CrossBooks, 2011), 53, 95–97.

2. Adapted from China Inland Mission, *The Obstinate Horse and Other Stories from the China Inland Mission* (Shoals, IN: Kingsley Press, 2004), chap. 1. See also, Mary K. Crawford, *The Shantung Revival* (The Revival Library at www.revival-library.org, based on the 1933 edition of Crawford's work), locs. 46–53, Kindle; and Dennis Balcombe, *China's Opening Door* (Lake Mary, FL: Charisma House, 2014), 27.

Finding Your Own Personal Bible Verses

1. Robert J. Morgan, *Reclaiming the Lost Art of Biblical Meditation* (Nashville: HarperCollins, 2017), xi.

Praying in Deep Water

1. Andrew Murray, *Daily Secrets of Christian Living: A Daily Devotional*, comp. Al Bryant (Grand Rapids: Kregel, 1978), July 4.
2. A. D. Hosterman, *Life and Times of James Abram Garfield* (Springfield, OH: Farm and Fireside Publishing Company, 1882), 53–54.

How Christ Came to Church

1. Condensed from Adoniram Judson Gordon, *How Christ Came to Church* (New York: Fleming H. Revell, 1896; Grand Rapids: Kregel, 2010), 28–30.
2. Gordon, 33–34.

Revival

1. Hester Rendall, quoted in Robert J. Morgan, *Worry Less, Live More: God's Prescription for a Better Life* (Nashville: Thomas Nelson, 2017), 45.
2. Wesley Duewel, *Revival Fire* (Grand Rapids: Zondervan, 1995), 133.
3. V. Raymond Edman, *Out of My Life* (Grand Rapids: Zondervan, 1961), 205.
4. Edman, 208.

The Invisible Man

1. Dick McLellen, *Warriors of Ethiopia* (n.p.: Dick McLellen, 2006), 48–49.
2. McLellen, adapted from chap. 5.

Embracing God's Presence When He Feels Far Away

1. Thomas Merton, *No Man Is an Island* (Boston: Shambhala, 2005), 250.
2. Randy Posslenzny, in discussion with the author in February 2018. Used with permission.
3. *The Works of Jonathan Edwards*, vol. 1, *Letters and Personal Writings*, ed. George S. Claghorn (New Haven, CT: Yale University Press, 1998), 730.

Refreshing People

1. This story is based on a conversation with Ruth Bell Graham at her home in May 1972. I have avoided using quotation marks because I did not record the conversation, but the dialogue is based on copious notes and my best recollection. Before her death she granted written permission for me to use any and all of this material, as well as additional notes in my files.
2. C. S. Lewis, "On the Reading of Old Books," *God in the Dock* (Grand Rapids: Eerdmans: 1970), 200.
3. From the hymn "Come, My Soul, Thy Suit Prepare," by John Newton, published in 1779.

God's Exceedingly Entertaining Creation

1. Jonathan Edwards, *A Treatise Concerning Religious Affections* (Philadelphia: James Crissy, 1821), xxv.
2. Edwards, xxvi.

3. William Revell Moody, *The Life of D. L. Moody* (New York: Fleming Revell, 1900), 581.

Into the Sand

1. F. W. Boreham, *The Other Side of the Hill* (London: The Epworth Press, 1954), 117–21.

2. Personal interview with the author in March 2018. Used with permission. The interviewee's name has been withheld.

Into the Light

1. Condensed from Maud Jeanne Franc, *Into the Light* (London: Sampson Low, Marston, Searle, & Rivington, 1885), 140–45.

Don't Lose Heart

1. Peggy J. Parks, *Joseph Lister* (Farmington Hills, MI: Blackbirch Press, 2005), 5–6.

The Unseen Friend

1. Lucy Larcom, *The Unseen Friend* (Boston: Houghton Mifflin, 1892), vii–viii.

2. See Robert J. Morgan, *Angels: True Stories* (Nashville: Thomas Nelson, 2011); and Morgan, *The Angel Answer Book* (Nashville: Thomas Nelson, 2015).

3. From Spurgeon's sermons, "Mr. Fearing Comforted," preached on April 3, 1859, and "The Ascension of Christ," preached on March 25, 1871, condensed.

Cheered by the Presence of God

1. Robert J. Morgan, *The Red Sea Rules* (Nashville: Thomas Nelson, 2014), x.

2. Elisabeth Elliot, *Secure in the Everlasting Arms* (Ann Arbor, MI: Vine Books, 2002), 49–50.

3. Elliot, 52.

4. George MacDonald, *Beautiful Thoughts*, arr. Elizabeth W. Dougall (New York: James Pott, 1894), 22–23.

5. Quoted by Virginia Reed in *Daily Cheer for All the Year* (n.p.: George W. Jacobs, 1895), 157.

About the Author

Robert J. Morgan is a writer and speaker who serves as the teaching pastor at The Donelson Fellowship in Nashville. He is the author of *The Red Sea Rules*, *The Strength You Need*, *Reclaiming the Lost Art of Biblical Meditation*, *Then Sings My Soul*, and many other titles, with more than 4.5 million copies in circulation. He is available to speak at conferences and conventions. He and his wife, Katrina, have three daughters and sixteen grandchildren. Contact him at www.robertjmorgan.com.

Visit http://robertjmorgan.com/AlwaysNear for a free downloadable study guide for individual and group use as well as for information about five video lessons designed for group instruction and interaction.

Reclaiming the Lost Art of
Biblical Meditation

Find True Peace in Jesus

ROBERT J. MORGAN

Do you long to deepen your intimacy with the Lord? To find a sense of soul-steadying peace? To develop emotional strength? Then you will need to pause long enough to be still and know He is God. Trusted pastor Robert Morgan leads us through a journey into biblical meditation.

The practice is as easy and portable as your brain, as available as your imagination, as near as your Bible, and the benefits are immediate. As you ponder, picture, and personalize God's Word, you begin looking at life through His lens, viewing the world from His perspective. And as your thoughts become happier and holier and brighter, so do you.